Advance Praise

Everywhere I Look, Ona Gritz's memoir, is a heartbreaking portrait of Angie, a young woman who never had the chance to thrive, and her adored and adoring sister Ona, whose quest for answers about Angie's murder means unlocking long-held family secrets. This beautifully crafted story is devastating and yet hopeful, a reminder that the truth really can set you free.

> — Jane Bernstein, award-winning author whose books include *The Face Tells the Secret* and *Bereft – A Sister's Story*

In this poignant memoir, written in the form of a letter to a lost sister, Ona Gritz grapples with the weight of family secrets and the profound impact they can have on our lives. In precise, poetic prose, Gritz explores the complexities of family dynamics and the ways in which her understanding of those dynamics shifts as she reckons with both the shock of her sister's tragic death and what she learns about her family and herself in its aftermath. *Everywhere I Look* is a testament to the love between sisters, the difficulty of understanding ourselves within the sometimes confusing context of our families, and the power of confronting the past to create the possibility of peace, and even forgiveness."

> — Andrea J. Buchanan, *New York Times* bestselling author of *Five-Part Invention* and *The Beginning of Everything*

Ona Gritz has smashed familial silence to pieces, and pulled the story of her beloved sister out of the wreckage and into the light. *Everywhere I Look* is a stunningly beautiful and fearless unraveling of one family's party line, and a testament to the deep love between sisters—still just as ardent, tender, and devoted decades beyond death.

> — Lilly Dancyger, author of *First Love* and *Negative Space*

Everywhere I Look is a profound and beautifully written memoir whose layers unfold to reveal a devastating series of family secrets and a grisly true crime tragedy. Gritz is masterful at recreating on the page the sister she lost, while illuminating the psychological complexity of family relationships.

— Helen Fremont, author of *The Escape Artist* and *After Long Silence*

Ona Gritz was a college student when her troubled, beautiful, vivid sister—a mother pregnant with a second child—was murdered. But it would take years before Gritz would begin to understand the complexities that surrounded that death and defined the years of living that came before. With a detective's determination and a poet's heart, Gritz explores matters of belonging (and not belonging), being loved and being lost, wishing for and wanting more. *Everywhere I Look* is testament and testimony, a sister's transformative journey toward bringing a heartbreaking past into the glimmering light.

— Beth Kephart, author of *Wife | Daughter | Self: A Memoir in Essays*

Everywhere I Look is part love story, part murder mystery, part coming-of-age memoir. Ona Gritz, in exquisite detail, examines her deep love for her older, adopted sister, a lost, wounded girl, who ultimately runs away—with tragic consequences. The longer Gritz digs into secrets surrounding her sister, the deeper her sadness—and the more urgent the prose. This memoir is courageously crafted like a love letter to her sister, a way to hold the absent sister close. This story of sister-love is a truly stunning and emotionally authentic exploration of sorrow and grief.

— Sue William Silverman, author of *How to Survive Death and Other Inconveniences*

This achingly gorgeous memoir - of yearning for a beloved, long-gone sister; coming to doubt fossilized family narratives; and pursuing with accelerating urgency a multitude of concealed truths - is enthralling, perspective-altering, and compassion-building. I will never stop thinking of its heart, and revelations, whenever a friend's family story reduces a relative to caricature, or I ponder a lost loved one whose depths remain inscrutable. And I will never stop admiring Ona Gritz - so brave with her honesty, so gifted with her pen, so open to uncovering, beneath opaque answers, the complex and poignant poetry of those dearest to us. This is a book that will take hold of your emotions - and, if you're willing, change you.

— Rachel Simon, *New York Times* bestselling author of *Riding the Bus with My Sister*

Everywhere
I Look

Everywhere
I Look

Ona Gritz

Apprentice
House Press
Loyola University Maryland

First Edition

Hardcover ISBN: 978-1-62720-507-8
Paperback ISBN: 978-1-62720-508-5
Ebook ISBN: 978-1-62720-509-2

Design by Lindsey Bonavita
Editorial Development by MK Barnes
Promotion Development by Ariana Mera

Published by Apprentice House Press

Apprentice
House Press
Loyola University Maryland

Loyola University Maryland
4501 N. Charles Street, Baltimore, MD 21210
410.617.5265
www.ApprenticeHouse.com
info@ApprenticeHouse.com

For Angie Boggs
July 26, 1956 - January 11, 1982
My sister. My first love.

*And the end of all our exploring will be to arrive where we started
and know the place for the first time.*
~T.S. Eliot

*But Angie, I still love you, baby
Everywhere I look I see your eyes...*
~Mick Jagger/Keith Richards

Chapter One

Angie, I'll begin on the evening of January 10, 1982, which is to say I'll begin with the ending. My last few hours as your sister. Your, Ray's, and baby Ray-Ray's last few hours at all. I'll place myself—nineteen, on winter break from college in New York—on the nubby plaid couch in your San Francisco apartment. You'd gone with Ray to run a quick errand. Ray-Ray was asleep in his crib in the back room. My friend Kay was with me, as was your friend Greg. And because I can write this down but can't change any of it, the Hendersons were there, too, in your small living room, the five of us watching an Errol Flynn movie on TV to pass the time until you returned.

I have been asked, over these many years, how I felt in the Hendersons' presence. Had I sensed anything menacing about them? Any hint at all that they were capable of smothering an infant, strangling a pregnant woman, shooting a man at close range with his own gun? My answer is always no. The Hendersons were likely broke and seemed unconventional, but that could be said of all the friends you introduced me to since you'd gone out on your own at sixteen. Mostly, what I remember is Philip crouched on the floor close to the TV, saying, "Tell me that good-looking blond-haired man doesn't always get his way," whenever Errol Flynn came on screen.

Philip was a good-looking man himself, lanky and muscular with wavy hair and small features. He also had more tattoos than I'd ever seen on one person. I put him at around twenty-five, like

1

you, though his wife Velma seemed much older—thin and wizened with a voice like she constantly needed to hold back a cough.

"Just look at that man with the pencil-thin mustache," Philip said as Errol Flynn swung from a mast in his tights and thigh-high boots.

Kay, too, sat on the floor, just below where I was on the couch, long hair swept over one shoulder, long legs hugged to her chest. Something she remembers from that night is Ray's parrot, perched in its cage squawking. But somehow, I've erased it. What I wish I could erase is my embarrassment over being stuck watching TV with these strangers while we waited for you and Ray to give us a ride back to the Victoria Hotel where Kay had a room. I also felt embarrassed by your wall hanging, Bugs Bunny on black velvet. "We got that for me, not the baby," you'd told us when we first came in that afternoon, and instead of smiling at the goofy sweetness of that admission, as I would have just the year before, I bristled. Three semesters of college behind me and I was now the arbiter of worthwhile art and good taste.

While I'm on regrets, I should have called you when I said I would the day before. After Kay picked me up at the airport, we went to Powell Street to watch the cable cars turn around and wound up chatting and people-watching through what was left of the afternoon. By the time we returned to Kay's room at the Victoria, it had grown dark.

"Now I feel bad," I confessed as I picked up the phone. "They were expecting to hear from me hours ago."

"Just say you tried before, and the line was busy," Kay suggested. "A little white lie won't hurt anyone."

It was Ray who answered. "That's not possible," he said coolly in response to my fib. "We've got a second line."

"On this number?" I looked up at Kay, who blushed along with me.

"Yeah, I can switch between them. What time did you call?"

"Early afternoon, I guess. Maybe I dialed wrong."

We made plans to meet the following day, and then Ray hung up without passing the phone to you or saying goodbye.

"Whoever heard of having two lines on one phone?" I moaned to Kay. The white lie that wasn't supposed to hurt anyone hurting Ray, hurting you, and, as I sit here forty years later, still hurting me.

Nonetheless, you came to meet me the next morning as promised.

"There they are," I told Kay when I spotted you approaching our meeting place in front of the Victoria. You pushed Ray-Ray's stroller, muttering under your breath as you teetered on spiky heels that I assumed hurt your feet. Beside you, Ray whispered, as though to calm you, while Greg loped along slightly behind, gazing over your heads.

"No kidding," Kay said.

For a moment, her response threw me, but then I saw the four of you through my friend's eyes and realized you were unmistakable. Ray, as kind and easygoing as he was, had a habit of narrowing his eyes at people, sizing them up. He was tall, of course, but Greg—that smoothly handsome Black man dressed all in white that day—was taller, towering over you, my defiantly pretty and very pregnant big sister.

In another fifteen years, nearly everyone between the ages of eighteen and thirty would have tattoos, but back then such markings were mostly reserved for bikers and marines. Still, a rose bloomed on one of your shoulders while the leaves of another flower peeked out from your significant cleavage. You wore a tight-fitting ribbed purple shirt, and I wondered, just as I had the year before, what pregnancy did to the legibility of the *Property of Big Bear* tattoo on your lower belly. Not to mention how Ray felt seeing that indelible declaration to an old boyfriend every time you undressed.

I remember how sunny and warm the day was. We headed to Golden Gate Park, you and Ray taking the baby in Ray's truck while Greg accompanied Kay and me on the bus. He talked the whole way, filling us in on revenge-filled dramas that involved people neither of us knew. Kay and I stole glances at each other, but Greg was too involved in his own stories to notice. When you'd introduced us the previous year, he was with his beautiful outgoing girlfriend, Charlie Ann, and had struck me as quiet and self-consciously polite. But, on this trip, Greg was alone, and I had a growing sense that he was interested in me.

At the park, Ray spread a blanket on the grass and supported you while you lowered yourself into a sitting position. I started to unbuckle Ray-Ray from his stroller, but you stopped me.

"It's easier if we leave him where he is."

I settled for poking Ray-Ray in the belly and tickling his chin, which made him laugh and kick his chubby legs.

"Greg was really excited to hear you were coming," you said, twisting your mouth into a sly smile. When Greg nodded, you told him, "My sister's not just cute. She's an A student."

"Actually, I don't get grades at my school," I corrected you. "Just evaluations."

"Oh. Well, anyway, she's the brains of the family."

Until that moment, I'd always loved to hear you brag about me. But your attempt to fix me up with Greg made me feel like you no longer knew me. And why would you when I hadn't shared much of myself with you in the last year? I'll tell you now that the guys I liked at SUNY Purchase were aspiring artists, poets, and intellectuals. That, when I'd arrived as a freshman the year before, I felt completely unsophisticated and discovered I was terribly under-read. I worked hard at catching up, reading late into the night, reviewing my notes between classes, smoothing out the harsh consonants and misplaced vowels of my Queens accent.

When summer came, I convinced Mom and Dad to let me fly to Boulder to study poetry at Naropa Institute. The friends I made there, including Kay, were serious writers, all older than me, who treated me like a prodigy and favored baby sister. Kay and I were roommates and, as we lay in our twin beds, like you and I had done when we were little, she reminisced about growing up with three older brothers. I told her about the many times you ran away and confided how lonely I'd felt during my long stretches as an only child while you lived a life on the streets I barely understood.

But now you had Ray and seemed settled and happy, mailing home photos of the two of you together, of Ray-Ray on his changing table, of you once again plump and pregnant in a nightgown Mom had sent. It felt so comforting to have an actual address and phone number where I could reach you. You almost seemed like other people's sisters.

Meanwhile, my focus was on becoming a real poet like Kay. When she and I planned this visit, we talked about going to City Lights Bookstore and Cloud House and bringing our poems to open readings. We'd get to do all that, I knew, starting the following day. But I was so caught up with who I wanted to be, for the first time ever in your company, I felt restless.

I asked again about releasing Ray-Ray from his stroller so he could crawl around, but you and Ray both thought it was a bad idea. "He'll just wind up getting into everything," you explained.

"Okay," I said, though he was such a calm baby, it didn't make sense to me. "You're a good little guy," I told him, rubbing his round belly. He grinned and pulled off his socks, revealing his eleven toes. It occurred to me that, as his poet auntie, I should write an extra line of "This Little Piggy" just for him.

"Maybe it's time *we* move around," Ray suggested. "Anyone hungry?"

He helped you up and pushed Ray-Ray's stroller out of the grass and onto a path that would take us to the street.

By then, of course, you and I had matching limps—mine from cerebral palsy, yours from that awful car accident a few years back. Now, we plodded along, falling behind the others. Alone for the moment, I felt my usual gush of love for you.

"Remember what you said about eating out when you first moved to San Francisco?" I asked.

"No, baby. What'd I say?"

"That you always picked restaurants that were uphill, so once you were full, you only had to walk down."

"Sounds like me." You roped your arm around my shoulder, and I buried my nose in your thick hair, breathing in the familiar mix of smoke and shampoo.

"Stop sniffing me," you said, laughing. "What are you, part wolf?"

We followed the others into a brightly lit coffee shop, where there was a short wait for a table. The couple ahead of us in line had a baby close to Ray-Ray's age.

"Why can't you be more like that?" Ray asked your boy. It wasn't the first time he'd teasingly criticized him, and it bothered me, even though Ray-Ray was too young to understand his daddy's words.

"What's wrong with being like that?" the other baby's father asked, nodding toward Ray-Ray, who was watching the glossy cakes turn in their round glass case.

From what I remember, Ray either didn't hear him or chose not to respond.

Finally, we were seated. While we studied our menus, you leaned over and whispered to me, "Kay's really nice. I can see why you like her so much."

My throat tightened at the generosity of your words. I knew Mom had told you on the phone that I was mostly coming to San Francisco to see Kay, my new friend who was a year older than you were.

"I wish you hadn't done that," I'd said when Mom relayed the conversation to me.

"You want her to give you the space to visit with Kay, don't you?"

I did, but I hated for you to feel like I was replacing you. Though, in a way, I was. Replacing you with girlfriends was something I learned to do early.

It was after lunch that we made our way to your place on Webster Street, Kay and I taking the bus again with Greg while you and Ray drove ahead. When you let us into the apartment, it surprised me to find another couple puttering around the living room.

You nodded to the Hendersons and made quick introductions. "They're staying with us for a while," you said.

Then, with Bugs Bunny and, apparently, a squawking parrot watching over us, we sat on the floor to admire a litter of new kittens.

You picked one up and let it squirm against your chest. "These are my babies," you said, and I thought back to the stray cats you brought home when we were little, when you were still Andra.

Mom, being Mom, wouldn't let them in the house, so we'd set up a box on the front porch. When it rained, you begged to bring them inside, but Mom always assured us they'd just go under the house and wait out the storm. Invariably, they disappeared.

"And The Cat Came Back," the two of us used to sing. But none of our cats ever did. Over time, I came to feel like the song was about you: my sister who'd grab a few things and disappear as I slept soundly across the room, but who could always be counted on to resurface eventually.

While we sat on the floor watching the kittens, Ray-Ray crawled over and took my arm so he could pull himself up to standing.

"If he annoys you, just push him down," you said, and I stared at you, shocked.

"He's fine," I answered, placing my arm protectively around his little torso.

Months later, I'd think of that moment of coolness toward your son, and the way Ray teased him, and find a small amount of comfort in those things. He'd have had a hard life, I told myself.

Chapter Two

In the two-family house in Far Rockaway where we grew up, there were stories I never questioned, odd as they were. That your birthmother named you after the Andrea Doria, a cruise ship that crashed and sank the day before you were born. That, six months later, when she gave you up for adoption, she didn't contact an agency or an orphanage. She perched on a stool in Dad's bar and offered you to him.

You were three when, for some reason, Mom chose to shorten your name. "From now on, you're Andra."

"My name's not At-a," you were famous in our family for having said. "My name is At-e-a."

Three years later, when our parents brought home a premature baby so tiny you mistook me for a doll, it was *my* name you found baffling.

"Ona?" you asked. "Like *own a* house?"

One hint that something wasn't quite right with my body was how, crawling, I moved myself forward with a palm and then followed it up with an elbow. The doctors explained to our parents that, either during my birth or soon after, damage was done to the part of the brain that controls motor function. When my mind sent messages to the left side of my body, my muscles read them clearly. But when it sent them to the right, the messages were somehow garbled, and the muscles only partially understood. At two, when I finally walked, I was wobbly and pigeon-toed. It took me even longer to start talking. But, though cerebral palsy can often affect speech, in my case, Mom simply jumped in to speak for me, quick to anticipate my needs.

It was you who got me, at almost three, to finally speak for myself. We were eating with our parents in the cafeteria of a department store when you announced, "After I finish my lunch, I'm going to eat Ona's."

I waited for Mom to notice and defend my food. When that didn't happen, I opened my mouth. "No, you had yours already," I said.

Is that my first memory of being your sister? Or does it just feel like a memory, the anecdote told to me so often I came to picture it in my mind? Here's another, almost as early, that I'm sure is my own.

I was on Mom's lap at the boardwalk, with you beside us on the bench. Mom had on a bra that made her breasts into padded pointy cones that struck me as the perfect place to rest my hands.

"Ooooh," you sang out, letting me know I'd done something embarrassing and naughty, and that you found it wonderfully entertaining.

"You can keep your hands there," Mom assured me. But you smirked, your eyes lit with mischief, and I understood that I'd tripped over to your side of the line. Already, at three and nine, our roles were clear to us. I was our parents' good girl. You were a devilish force. Your delight told me there must be something bad having to do with touching and girlhood and parts of the body. I dropped my twig-thin arms to my sides.

You teased, fibbed, and wandered off from the safe circle of neighborhood blocks where we were allowed to play when all the parents were inside. I was the daughter who did as I was told. But I believed it was more than obedience that made me good. Goodness lived inside me. A pure, quiet taste somewhere in the middle of my body, light and clean like vanilla ice cream. If I had to guess what lived inside you, I'd say it was something quick and blistering. Those firecrackers kids set off by throwing them to the pavement as hard as they can.

"If you say to Andra, 'wait right here' and step away for a minute, she'll be five blocks away by the time you get back," I once heard Dad tell Uncle Manny. "But if you say the same thing to Ona, she won't even breathe."

"Have you ever tasted an onion?" you asked me one night at supper.

"I don't think so." I glanced at Mom for confirmation, but she was busy telling Dad something in Yiddish.

"Oh, you'd like it," you went on, drawing me close by speaking quietly. "But you have to take a really big bite."

I reached for the white globe that sat on the table, peeled and ready for slicing.

"Ma-Mee..." I cried a moment later, mouth numb, chest scorched from inside.

But once it was over, the fiery taste a memory in my mouth, the onion became a story. When I told it to the kids in the playground, I wasn't telling it *on* you. I was bragging. My sister is fun and funny, I felt the story said. To me, you were the brightest light in our house.

Remember the nights we danced on our beds with pajama bottoms on our heads as our long flowing hair? "Try this," you'd say, waving your arms for the Monkey, or corkscrewing your body downward, nose held, for the Swim. I'd do my best to imitate you, and if my movements were clumsy and stiff, you never let on. We'd play at being go-go girls until Mom came to tuck us in.

"We can still play from bed if we're quiet," you whispered one night, though we weren't supposed to talk after lights out.

"We'll get in trouble," I whispered back. By *we* I meant *you*. I'd never been in trouble.

"You know..." you went on, "there are monsters watching. If we don't play, they're going to get us."

After that, the monsters were always there to oversee us. Sometimes it was the girl monsters who would let us sleep. "They're nicer," you explained. But most often, the boy monsters were in charge and they made us play. I grew to prefer them and their insistence that we keep our game going, but I never said so aloud.

Another of Mom's rules was no getting out of bed except to use the bathroom.

"Come lay with me," you whispered anyway.

That was back when I had to wear a leg brace and heavy shoe to bed and, as quiet as I tried to be crossing the room, it bumped against the floor. Sometimes, no one noticed, and I got to stay next to you, snuggling until we felt sleepy. Other times, Mom or Dad heard the thump and called sternly, "What was that?"

"Ona fell out of bed again," you'd always call back.

"Have you really been falling out of bed?" Mom finally asked after you left for school one morning.

Sitting at the table eating Lucky Charms, I felt an awful push-pull inside me, a tug-o-war with Mom on one end of the rope and you on the other. She, we both knew, always believed me. "Tell Mommy..." you often said, as in "Tell Mommy you like it," when you coaxed me into sitting with you during *Dark Shadows*, a show so scary you couldn't bear to watch it alone. Now, staring down at the mess of pastel colors in my bowl, I muttered my answer. That night, Dad placed a chair with its back against my bed to keep me safe.

I missed sneaking over for those nighttime cuddles, but we still had other rituals I loved, including our summer strolls to the playground while Mom made supper.

"Don't push too high," I'd remind you as you helped me onto a swing.

"I promise, baby."

But that firecracker inside you sometimes went off, and you'd pull back as hard as you could on the chains.

"Hey. Don't!"

Then you'd do the thing that frightened me most, raise the swing above your head so that, released, it veered wildly. I'd hold on so tight, tears streamed down my cheeks.

"You promised!" I'd yell once you finally captured and stilled it.

"I was just playing with you," you'd say, stroking my hair. "Don't tell, okay?" I never did. After all, you always saved me in the end. My tormentor and my protector, the back and forth of it as dizzying as my ride on the swings.

"Touch tongues?" you'd ask later, before we let ourselves back in the house.

I'd stick out my tongue and tap it to yours for an instant. This ritual of ours as private as the time we pricked our fingers, pressed blood-to-blood, and became sisters for real.

Chapter Three

While we were in Golden Gate Park, or at lunch, on what would turn out to be your last afternoon, a woman who would only identify herself as a friend of yours called our house in Far Rockaway. She told Mom that you and Ray were in some kind of trouble and that "Angie's little sister should stay away."

"But she's there already," Mom said.

"I know. Right now, she's on a date with a large Black man."

A while later, the woman called back, insisting Mom at least tell me to stay away from the Jack in the Box where you, Ray, and your friends hung out.

"Something's going on," she warned.

Mom and I finally spoke the next morning.

"I don't know what that was about," I said, feeling baffled but not too concerned. "We saw Angie and Ray yesterday, and everyone's fine."

"Were you on a date with a Black man?"

"No, Mom. She was probably talking about Angie's friend Greg. We all spent time together yesterday."

When we hung up, Kay and I wondered aloud who would have made those bizarre calls. I had the vaguest sense that I should ask if you and Ray needed help or money, figuring I could present your case to Dad if necessary. But I wasn't ready to give that much credence to what the anonymous caller had to say.

"I think it has to be the woman who's staying with them," Kay said. "Angie probably told her she was hoping to fix you up with

Greg."

"Maybe." I got up and stood before the dresser mirror, flicking a pick through my new perm. "So how old would you say that woman is anyway?"

"Fifty-something?" She joined me at the mirror and ran her fingers through her blond hair. "Definitely old enough to be that guy's mother."

"I think it's kind of cool they're a couple. They're certainly breaking stereotypes."

What I wanted to say was that seeing Philip and Velma together—an attractive man married to a woman who was far from beautiful—made me hopeful since I felt far from beautiful myself. But I knew if I tried to express that to Kay, she'd dismiss my insecurities.

"Guys always like you," she told me often during our summer in Boulder, but I didn't believe that about myself. It was you, my outgoing, voluptuous sister, who left a trail of guys behind you. You were sex and adventure and, though we both now limped, I would forever be your scrawny, handicapped little sister.

Still, there was no denying that, while we all watched Errol Flynn, Greg had mostly watched me. I might have been flattered, but he'd pushed so hard, boasting about all the wrong things, until his handsome gaze made me uncomfortable enough to wish he hadn't come. Years later, though, Kay would pose the theory that his presence actually saved our lives.

"He grew quiet and alert as soon as we entered the apartment and he saw the Hendersons there. I think he stayed to protect you."

"Promise you'll call me tomorrow," you'd said that night as the four of us crammed into Ray's truck to drive back to the Victoria. You said it again when we all climbed out to hug goodbye.

"Aren't you going to hug Kay?" You nudged Ray, and he shyly complied. "Don't forget to call, baby," you said to me, giving me one last squeeze.

"I'll call," I'd promised. But now, once again, I put it off. There was so much Kay and I wanted to do with our day.

We headed to City Lights, where we sat on the floor reading to each other from slim volumes of poetry. Afterwards, we went for tacos in the Mission District and stayed late talking and jotting snippets of overheard conversation in our notebooks to work into poems later.

When we returned to the Victoria, so I could finally give you a call, it was already evening, and Ray was home from work.

He picked up on the first ring. "Have you heard from her?" he asked.

"No." I tightened my grip on the receiver. "She's not home?"

"I don't know where she is." He sounded truly worried.

"Does she have the baby with her?"

"No. He's here, sleeping. I've been calling around, and no one's seen her."

"What about your roommates? Were they there when she left?"

"Yeah, they said she got a call sometime this afternoon and took off right after. Let me get back to you. I want to try a few more people."

When I didn't hear back after half an hour, I called him again. This time, Ray told me that Ray-Ray was with you after all.

"Wait a minute," I said. "She came to get him?"

"No, I was wrong. I thought he was sleeping in our room, but she had him all along. Hold on a sec," Ray said, and I heard the muffled sound of voices. "I don't understand it," he continued, back on the line. "Her purse is here. She doesn't have any money."

I glanced out the window at the cars zooming past. "She probably just stepped out," I said.

Kay and I had planned to go to the movies that night, but decided to stay in, close to the phone. I tried your number several more times, but now no one picked up.

"That's strange," Kay commented when there was still no answer at midnight. "Doesn't Ray have to work in the morning?"

I couldn't reach you the following day either, of course, though I tried every few hours. Kay thought we should contact the police.

"You don't understand. My sister always does stuff like this." I described the time Mom and I were visiting and you snuck out while we were asleep in our hotel room. "She left her pants under the bed and stole my jeans," I told Kay. "We were leaving that day, and she never even came back to say goodbye."

"Yeah, but that was before Ray, right? Now she's got the baby and she's *so* pregnant."

"True," I said. Still, I somehow believed that you were punishing me for not calling when I said I would the day before, which, it occurs to me all these years later, wouldn't have been like you at all.

Usually, Kay kept her car parked in one spot and traveled around the city on cable cars and buses. But, now that we couldn't get you and Ray on the phone, she drove me to Jack in the Box, despite the warning Mom had gotten from your mysterious friend.

We found Greg eating with friends in a back booth. When I told him I couldn't reach you and Ray, he left his half-finished burger and followed Kay and me outside.

"It's weird," he said. "No one's seen them. I'm about ready to go looking."

I felt a twist in my stomach. Maybe this wasn't just a trick for my benefit.

"You know, I've got friends in the Hell's Angels and I'm sure they'd help us find them." Greg put his hand on my shoulder. "You can ride with me on my bike. All I need to do is make one call."

"What do you think?" I asked, turning to Kay.

"Thanks, but we'll look ourselves," she told Greg.

When we were a block away, Kay gave me a shove. "Like I was really going to let you ride off on that guy's motorcycle."

We wandered the neighborhood for a while, drifting into coffee shops and approaching people on park benches I thought might be acquaintances of yours.

You know, this wasn't the first time I'd roamed that hilly city in search of you. Do you remember, when I was maybe fifteen, Mom, Dad, and I had plans to come to San Francisco? We'd talked to you and made arrangements, but days before we were scheduled to fly out, you dropped out of touch. The number you'd given us was no longer in service, and you never called. We went anyway, since Tina still lived in the city then, and I carried your picture with me everywhere, showing it to bus drivers, waiters, and musicians on the street. "Have you seen this girl? Have you seen her?"

"That's enough, Ona," Dad finally said.

"Stop worrying," Mom put in. "We know she does this."

Now, on the phone, she said it again.

"They probably ran out on the rent. Don't worry. Andra always turns up, like a bad penny."

It won't surprise you to hear that this was something she often said. Ordinarily, the coldness of it bothered me. But now I found solace in the familiar phrase. This was us. You disappeared. I fretted. Our parents simply waited. You surfaced again.

"Don't let it ruin your trip," Mom told me, and I decided it was good advice.

Over the next few days, Kay and I ate shrimp at Fisherman's

Wharf, drove down the crazy curves of Lombard Street, and brought our poems to open readings. In one coffee house, a tiny, elderly woman in old-fashioned clothes stepped behind the podium, and all we could see as she read was her pillbox hat.

"That'll be you in sixty years," Kay, who was eight inches taller than me, teased.

Still, each day, every few hours, I interrupted whatever we were doing to find a payphone and try your number. I'd press the receiver to my ear and listen as it rang and rang.

On my last night in California, I lay in bed and recalled my final conversation with Ray.

"She probably just stepped out," I'd said, my second white lie to him in as many days.

"This isn't like her," Ray told me, but I knew better.

I thought of the guy you had lived with, back in New York, who worked for Kentucky Fried Chicken. How, one day, he came home and found that his stereo and other valuables were gone, and so were you. He walked into the kitchen and saw that, before you left, you'd served lunch to the thieves. The chicken bones were still on the table.

As I write this, I realize that I don't know your side of that story. It was one of so many things I never thought to ask you about. But the version I'd heard—second hand? third?—allowed me to believe, for just a little while longer, that even though you, Ray, and little Ray-Ray were missing, nothing was terribly wrong.

Chapter Four

"Everyone's got something," Mom used to tell me when she buckled my leg brace at night or sat with me while I tried to tell coins from stones in my numb palsied hand.

Everyone's got something. You and I certainly understood the truth in that, just by living in our house. Think of the pills Dad took for his jangled nerves, and how it often seemed like it was the two of us who jangled them. Remember the time you and I played in the backyard while he worked on putting together a kiddie pool for me? I came too close and squealed too loudly, and he poked his eye with a rod he was trying to install. After that, if Mom asked him to watch us, he refused, saying, "I'm not a babysitter."

For a time, we weren't allowed to talk during dinner because our chatting and giggling bothered him while he ate. We created a game out of trying to stay silent, but that just made us laugh, so Mom began feeding us earlier on our own.

Dad was also afraid about money, though when I asked Mom if we were rich or poor, she always answered that we were *comfortable*. Nonetheless, Dad walked into town to pay our bills so he wouldn't have to use up our stamps and said no to any toys he'd have to keep buying batteries for.

One thing Mom seemed afraid of was dirt. We weren't allowed to play in the sandbox, wear our shoes in the house, or even go into the living room with its red rug, velvet loveseats, and breakable knick-knacks. From the easy-clean vinyl couch in the TV area, we watched Mom wipe off the bottom of her socks before entering the forbidden zone to do her dusting.

"Ma ought to get one of those velvet ropes like in museums," you joked the one time we snuck in, walking on our knees so we wouldn't leave telltale marks on the carpet.

Another of Mom's *somethings* was her voice, which could turn into a screech when she laughed, gossiped, or called to us from another room. She never got mad at me, but when she yelled at you or Dad, she used her witch voice, sharp and shrill.

Of course, one of your *somethings* was epilepsy. I remember waking one morning to a sound like someone gently gargling. Across the room, you slept with your mouth open, vomit flowing onto your pillow the way water spills from a garden hose right after it's turned off.

"Andra! You're throwing up!" When you didn't respond, I called, "Mommy!" truly frightened now. "Ma!"

Mom came in and wiped your mouth with a damp washcloth, then placed a face towel beneath your cheek. "Andra's having a seizure," she explained as you slept on.

"What?" you asked when you finally woke up. "What are you staring at?"

But your biggest *something*, it seemed to me then, was how you couldn't help getting in trouble. You'd say a bad word, or get caught lying, and wind up with a bar of soap in your mouth. You'd sit on me and fan your hair over my belly until my laughter turned to wails, and then have to kneel in the kitchen, the cutout specks in the linoleum leaving a pattern of rough red marks on your knees.

In my memory, these punishments were always meted out by Mom, Dad either at his job in the subway control tower or sleeping behind a closed door after a late shift the night before.

A *something* I carry to this day is that, for the few years you and I lived together in that house—sleeping in the same yellow room, eating together at the round dinette table, sitting pressed up against each other watching TV—it felt as though we had two very different moms. Mine put fresh socks on my feet before they touched the cold floor on winter mornings and read picture books to me in the bathroom when I had trouble going. In the story she told of my birth, a nurse woke her up to tell her she'd had a girl and Mom answered, "You're just saying that to make me happy." Yet, the woman who raised you before my eyes often seemed like she was made of rage. Once, she even chased you through the house and beat you with the dustpan.

I want to say the fight started while I was in the backyard with Lisa from upstairs, who'd brought out her new Barbie with bendable legs. If Lisa had a *something*, it was that we sometimes hated her because her father worked for Mattel, and she got these treasures before they even made it to the stores.

"Take her out of the box," I'd pleaded. "Let's play."

The doll behind the cellophane smiled at me, and I ached to hold her by her impossibly thin waist, but Lisa was content to gaze at that box like it was a painting.

"I want to keep her nice for a while," she said.

Is that really what I was doing before I went inside to find you and Mom both screaming on that long-ago afternoon? Who knows? But it's one of so few memories I have of our upstairs neighbor, who was seven that spring when I was five and you, at eleven, had never lived anywhere but home. What I'm certain of is that, right after I slipped into our room, you burst in and landed on your bed. In a flash, Mom was there, the copper dustpan behind her back so you couldn't see it. She held it over her head a moment and then began pummeling your thighs.

"Stop!" I screamed, but she didn't seem to notice me there in the room.

When it was finally over, I climbed onto your bed and did most of the crying.

"I wanted to stop her," I sobbed.

"It's alright," you said as you stared at the ceiling. "It's okay."

I looked at the welt forming on your leg and thought of the baby doll I'd inherited from you that had magic-marker circles on its butt cheeks. "Her tushy's blue," you'd explained, "from a spanking."

Everyone's got something. One thing I assumed every family had was a most beloved child.

"You're your mom's favorite, right?" I quietly asked my friend Dina one afternoon as we sipped water from the tiny cups in her plastic tea set.

Dina had brothers. Aaron, a pale boy who lazed around watching cartoons whenever I was over, and Eli, the first homely infant I'd ever seen.

"My mother loves us all equally," Dina pronounced.

I didn't understand. "But you're the only girl," I reminded her. "You know you're the favorite secretly..."

I glanced over at Aaron lying on the floor watching *Rocky and Bullwinkle.* He had a cold and kept snuffling the gunk from his nose back upward with snorts that made my chest hurt.

"No," Dina insisted. "My mom has enough love in her heart for all of us."

I stopped asking, figuring her mother said those things just to sound nice.

A few days later, you and I sat in the TV area, playing Monkees albums. We had four, but I made a point of saying *Pisces, Aquarius, Capricorn & Jones* was mine alone since Dad had given it to me when my tooth fell out.

"They're all ours equally," you said.

I felt a twinge, aware that little, if anything, was really equal between us. Still, my tooth had come out and, instead of a made-up fairy leaving me quarters, Dad had presented me with the album as a gift.

"It's mine and you have to ask my permission if you want to play it," I declared, sure Mom would take my side if you complained. Part of me felt awful, knowing that I held that power. And yet, I found myself wielding it and unable to back down, even as I saw the hurt wash over your face. My love, it seemed, like yours, was tinged with danger.

Still, it wasn't long before we were sweet with each other again. Out in the backyard, we tied a long jump rope to the garage door, and I turned it while you practiced double Dutch moves. Afterwards, we lay close together in the grass, flipping through magazines.

"Davy Jones got married," you told me, showing me an article in *Tiger Beat*.

"Oh, no! I asked him in my letter to wait!"

Lucky for you, the guy you liked wasn't a famous TV star who lived a million miles away. It was just Michael, Lisa's older brother, who lived right above us. When Lisa came out, you asked if he was home.

She nodded. "Yeah, there's a Mets game on."

Your face lit with your wild-girl grin. "Come here," you said, and led us to the bench on the edge of the driveway. "Okay. Let's sing "Michael Row Your Boat" as loud as we can and see if we can get him to stick his head out and notice us."

In just a few weeks, Lisa would dart from between parked cars and become God's neighbor, a ghost-girl, a *something* that haunted all of us.

But, for the moment, I sat between the two of you. Our faces raised in the sun as we aimed our *hallelujahs* toward an open upstairs window. Your thigh and Lisa's solid and warm against mine.

Chapter Five

Soon after I got home from San Francisco, I returned to SUNY Purchase for the spring semester. On March 1, I made my way to the campus library. Forcing myself to walk past the bustling periodical room, I climbed the stairs to the quiet of the top floor. There, I settled into a soft chair and opened Tillie Olsen's *Tell Me a Riddle,* the assigned reading for my women's lit course.

"I will sell the house anyway," the elderly man, in the title story of the collection, threatened his wife. His one wish was to move to a retirement community. "I am putting it up for sale. There will be a way to make you sign."

Do you recognize that voice? He sounded just like Dad who, long retired from his job at New York City's Transit Authority, had started lobbying for a winter home near Fort Lauderdale. He was actually there at that moment, visiting Uncle Manny, who had recently been diagnosed with cancer.

"I hate Florida," Mom spat whenever he brought it up. "There's no one there but old Jewish people."

"We're old Jewish people!"

"Speak for yourself, Lenny. I only see one altacocker here."

Like Dad, the husband in "Tell Me a Riddle" escaped the battleground by watching TV.

"Maybe you should just move there without me," Mom offered.

"Mrs. Live Alone and Like It," the husband in "Tell Me a Riddle" called his wife.

Reading, I felt an odd mix of embarrassment and homesickness.

At the same time, I felt inspired. Could I write with such elegance about our inelegant family?

When I left the library, I drifted toward the dorms to call home, as I'd done almost daily, hoping for news of you.

Mom picked up on the first ring. "I finally heard something," she said.

"You heard from Angie? Really?"

"Afraid not." She was using her receptionist voice. Serious. Efficient. "Are you sitting down?"

"Yes," I lied, pacing as much as the phone cord allowed. "So, who called?"

"The San Francisco police. Ray was shot."

"Oh no!" I leaned back against the desk, suddenly lightheaded, my palsied arm tightening against my chest. "Is he okay?"

"No, Ona, Ray's dead."

"What?" I stared at the metal bunk beds across from me. My rumpled blanket tossed to the floor. The sheets creased from my sleep. "When?"

"They just found him, but they can tell he's been dead for six weeks."

That had to be wrong. "I talked to him six weeks ago. He picked up the phone. Twice."

"He must have been killed right after."

Ray's dead, I told myself, trying to believe it. Ray's dead, trying to make it not be true. "What about Angie? Where's she?"

"No one knows. I'm starting to think she's probably dead too..."

"What?" I snapped, cutting her off.

"It's not like her not to call."

"She always turns up. You said so. 'Like a bad penny,' remember?"

"I know, honey, but..." She sighed. "You're right. She'll turn up. Call me back tomorrow, and I'll let you know if I've heard anything."

Angie, this is something I'd rather not tell you, but it wouldn't be right to leave it out. As much as I cared for Ray, over the next few weeks, whenever I felt the pull of grief, I'd work on erasing him. What I needed was for him to become paper-thin, like the few photos that were all I had of him. I did this so that his murder wouldn't hurt so much and, also, as a way to keep you alive. I convinced myself that you were on the lam. That you'd fallen for some other guy, and Ray's death was the heartbreaking result of a battle between the two men. Mom was right that it wasn't like you not to call, but it was like you to be protective. You'd inspired this crime of passion and were doing your best not to involve us.

"Accept any collect calls you get," I instructed Mom.

Dad was still away when I came home for spring break.

One evening, while I was foraging in the fridge for a snack, the phone rang. I picked it up and heard a man sobbing on the other end.

"Who are you trying to reach?"

The man couldn't catch his breath to answer.

"Who is this?" I tried again.

"Ray Boggs," he managed. A cold stone landed in my stomach. This couldn't be Ray Boggs. Ray was dead. "I'm Ray's father," he got out. "I just heard on the news."

"Oh, I'm so sorry."

"You knew? When did you know?"

I wasn't sure what to say. "Let me put my mother on the phone." I found Mom in the TV area, hemming a pair of jeans for me. "It's Ray's father. I feel so bad for him."

She got up slowly and went into the kitchen. I took her place on the couch and put a few crooked stitches in my pants. At first, I could hear her end of the conversation, but soon all I heard was my own blood pumping in my ears.

Fourteen years earlier, I'd sat in that same room, watching cartoons, when I pieced together from snatches of anxious phrases that someone in the upstairs half of our house had died. I tried to ask Mom about it, but all she'd tell me was, "We had a little accident." She was rinsing a sponge in the sink as she said it. Yet, somehow, I knew I was right. I knew this wasn't just a spilled glass of juice. When I kept asking questions, she sent me back to watch TV.

It was you who finally filled me in. Afraid the ice cream truck would leave, Lisa had rushed out into the street to get to it. I kept thinking it was the ice cream man who ran her over. But no, it was someone in a passing car.

"I saw her in the street, and she was all blue," you told me later that night, crying into my shoulder. "We were this close," you added, showing me two crossed fingers.

Usually, you held me. Usually, if we talked before bed, you made me sneak to your side of the room. But that night, too baffled and frightened to be sad, I was the big sister, wrapping my skinny arms around your broad shoulders, letting you curl up with me in my bed.

Now, Mom hung up with Ray's dad and came back to where I sat staring at a blank TV, my new jeans sprawled and empty on my lap.

I'd like to think I imagined what came next, or that it darkened in my mind over time. But I've read that "pain engraves a deeper memory," and this is a moment that's carved into my bones. "Well, she's dead," Mom announced with a crisscross slap of her hands, as though wiping them clean of you forever.

Chapter Six

It seemed like I just woke up one morning and you had the beginnings of a curvy figure and long hair that Mom sometimes helped you iron straight. Twelve years old, you didn't need to put pajama bottoms on your head and pretend anymore. In real life, you were pretty.

"Don't tell anyone," you said one night as you examined your waist in the closet mirror. "But I think I might be pregnant."

I stared at you, shocked. By now you had described to me, many times, exactly what people did to make babies.

"You should see your face," you said, grinning at me through the glass. "I'm not pregnant. I'm just playing with you."

For a moment, I felt relieved. But I could never tell with you what was true. What if you really were pregnant, I wondered. Would your baby be given away like you'd been? Is that what they'd make you do?

"Don't tell, okay?"

You'd say this when you folded the waistband of your skirt to make it shorter, or if you stopped to talk to a group of boys on our way home from Milty's where we bought button candy and wax lips. Often, I found you in the bathroom at the back of the house, puffing on a Kool. You'd have slid the small window open so our parents couldn't smell what you were up to, even though Dad smoked too. His hugs scented sweet with tobacco from the mirrored cans we used to catch fireflies in summer. His pipe cleaners dirty from the job they were named for, not shaped into flowers and jewelry like ours.

"I ever catch you with one of these, I'll kill you," you'd warn, flicking ashes into the toilet.

"You won't," I'd promise solemnly, thrilled to be in on your secrets.

There was a closet in that same bathroom where Mom hid our Hanukkah presents among the extra rolls of toilet paper and boxes of toothpaste. It's also where she kept an envelope filled with black-and-white photos of Tina and Steve as children in 1950's style clothes. Sometimes, you'd take them down from their high shelf and we'd look through them until we came to the few where they were already teenagers, and you and I, at seven and less than a year old, were with them at their house in Las Vegas. Mom had told us that their dad, Gene, was her cousin. But I couldn't think of a great aunt or uncle to connect them. Plus, it didn't really explain why Tina looked so remarkably like me.

As it was, most of our relatives were strangers to us, thanks to fights that had happened before I was born. Mom's brother wasn't speaking to her. Dad and his sister weren't speaking to each other. And Manny, the one uncle we knew well, had two daughters who weren't speaking to him. When I told Mom I thought it was sad that I didn't know my cousins, she said, "They're much older than you anyway." I wondered if she meant they wouldn't like me if they did know me, and worried that if this were true of them, it could someday be true of you too.

"Where's-my-sis-ter?" I asked one afternoon, bouncing a pink rubber ball in rhythm to the question. On TV, the 4:30 movie was about to start. You were usually home from school in time to watch it with me.

Mom sat at the dinette table, browsing *The Pennysaver*. "Probably out with friends."

I went to our room and flipped on the radio. Your favorite songs kept coming on: "Hey Jude," "Young Girl," "Yummy, Yummy, Yummy." But you still didn't walk in the door. During a newsbreak, I turned the radio off and pulled my homework from my book bag, a worksheet with common nouns and people's names in a jumble. The assignment was to pick out the names and circle them. I penciled a loop around *Susan*, your middle name, and around *John* and *Betty*. When I came to *Many*, I thought of Uncle Manny who called me monkey and said funny things by accident, like when he told Mom not to "make an assembly out of it" after she yelled at him for walking through her living room in shoes. *Many*. I circled the word, half-sure it was his name.

"Supper," Mom called.

"Where's Andra?" I asked, slipping into the seat across from Dad.

He glanced at Mom. "We're beginning to wonder," Dad said.

If our parents called your friends to see if anyone knew where you'd gone, or contacted the police when you still weren't home at bedtime, they didn't do it in my presence.

"Where do you think she is?" I asked Mom as she buckled the straps of my night brace.

"We don't know, honey, but I'm not worried. Everybody loves Andra. She'll be fine."

Lying alone in our room, I thought of all the relatives our parents no longer knew or were loved by, and wondered if she meant someone else would adopt you now, making you theirs. I also thought about a morning, just days before, when I woke to find you kneeling on my bed, your face so close to mine I felt your breath on my skin.

"Kiss me," you'd commanded, more like a leading man in a movie than a sister.

Something about it frightened me, so I'd curled up as tight as I could to put space between us.

"They turned you against me, didn't they?" you hissed, pressing your face even closer. "Go ahead and say it. They turned you against me."

"Nuh-uh, I love you," I protested, in tears. "I'm not against you."

"Yeah, right," you said and left me crying in my bed, not sure why I hadn't wanted to kiss you, not wanting to be one of the *theys* who were against you.

"Maybe she joined the circus," my friend Natalie suggested after you'd been gone a whole school week.

We were crouched by the side of her house, doodling in the dirt with sticks. "Why do you think that?"

She shrugged. "That's what people do when they run away."

"I guess."

"You know who knows where she is," Natalie continued.

"Who?"

She glanced toward the sky, then gave me a meaningful look, letting me know she meant Lisa.

"Yeah. She can see everyone everywhere."

Too soon, Natalie was called in for supper. Strolling home, I pulled leaves from the shrubs I passed and tore holes in them with my nails, making perfect slits on either side of the stems like tiny quarter moons. I was putting off another long night in our too-quiet house where your bed stayed neatly made and the only laughter was the tinny kind that came from sitcoms. But when I walked in the door, you were there, in the kitchen, talking to our parents in a hushed adult tone.

"You're back!" I meant to say as I ran to you. Instead, I burst into tears.

"Hey baby, I thought you'd be happy to see me."

I climbed onto your lap, wanting to tell you again that I wasn't against you. But all I could do was bury my face in your hair. It smelled of shampoo, smoke, and something unfamiliar, a combination of home and the wide outside world.

"Andra, were you in the circus?" I asked that night as we lay in our beds.

"Yeah, right," you snorted. "I was hired as a dancing bear."

"That's what Natalie thought," I mumbled, embarrassed. "So where were you?"

"Can we just go to sleep now, baby?" you said. "I'm really tired."

After that, running away became another *something* you did. In your absence, I asked Mom to play Barbies. But the one time she did, I had to tell her when to have her doll speak and even what to say. After that, I just played all the parts alone. Mom and I listened to albums together, though. Mostly soundtracks to musicals like *My Fair Lady*, *Oliver*, and *West Side Story*. We also played Old Maid and Mad Libs, and she read to me from *Kids Say the Darndest Things*. Once in a while, if I pestered her enough, she'd inspect my bare feet and let me into the off-limits living room where I'd gaze at the glass house that held her delicate nameless doll with its flowered kimono and face as white as a marshmallow. A gift from such a faraway place I couldn't imagine it, any more than I could imagine where you might be.

When you'd finally return, filling the house again with rock songs, secret cigarettes, and late-night whisper sessions, I no longer asked where you were or what you'd been up too. There was home and there was elsewhere. I didn't know how to think about elsewhere.

"I'm going to run away tonight," you confided in me one night. "When you wake up in the morning, I'll be gone."

You'd never given a warning before and, as I stared at you cross-legged on your bed, calmly combing your hair, I felt my throat close up and my right arm rise and tighten.

"Come on, Andra, you're just saying that."

Earlier that evening, we'd all watched *The Wizard of Oz* on TV. Right after Dorothy said, "Oh, Auntie Em, there's no place like home," Mom had turned to you with a pointed look. "See?"

"I know, Ma," you'd responded, which somehow made me think you were home to stay.

"Fine, don't believe me," you told me now.

"Don't go, Andra. Please?"

You stretched out under the covers and switched off the lamp. "Sorry, baby. I've already made plans."

I thought maybe, if I stayed awake, I could stop you from sneaking out. But the heaviness of that responsibility pulled me into a thick, dreamless sleep. When I finally woke, a bright sun lit up our yellow walls.

Across the room, your bed stood rumpled and empty. I dragged myself to the kitchen to tell Mom you were gone, but when I got there, I found you at the table pouring yourself a bowl of Cap'n Crunch. You put a finger to your lips and nodded toward the basement door to let me know Mom was down there in listening range.

"I thought you were leaving," I whisper-yelled, climbing onto the chair beside you. "You scared me."

You grinned and pushed my hair out of my eyes. "Come on,

baby. You knew I was goofing."

"I didn't," I insisted. Then I thought maybe I should have. You often said things just to scare me. Once you told me a killer had escaped from the mental hospital, Creedmoor. "He creeps around looking in windows for little girls to have for a midnight snack," you'd said. But when I pulled my blanket off the bed so I could sleep on the floor out of the madman's view, you'd laughed. "I'm only playing with you, silly."

"So, you're not going to run away tonight? Promise?"

"Pinky swear," you said, kissing your little finger.

But I found out the next morning you didn't mean it.

"She'll probably come back," Natalie said as we sat on the playground swings after school, twisting just enough to hear the chains squeak. "She always has, so far."

So far. Two tiny words that made a quick double sound. Like *Ona.* Like *Andra.* I thought of Dorothy in the movie telling her dog about a place "far, far away."

"So far," I repeated, lying belly-down on the swing and scudding my feet backwards so the ground moved, and Natalie couldn't watch me try not to cry.

Chapter Seven

The morning after we learned from Ray's dad that you and the baby had also been killed, I woke to find the house empty. I called down the basement steps and checked the backyard, then phoned the real estate office where Mom worked part-time as a receptionist.

"You went in?" I asked, incredulous.

"Well, I didn't see what good sitting around the house would do."

Maybe she was right, I decided. We weren't the kind of family to perch on cardboard boxes with the mirrors covered for a week. Still, anything I thought to do once we hung up—take a shower, eat breakfast—seemed disrespectful somehow.

Finally, I rooted around in the fridge for a stalk of celery to smear with cream cheese, a snack I wasn't especially fond of, but you had once loved. She'll never eat anything again, I thought and climbed back into bed.

In the days that followed, Mom stuck to her routine: work in the mornings, aerobics class in the afternoons, reading and needlepoint followed by TV in the evenings. I had no idea how to spend the time, so I slept a lot, curled up on top of the covers and wrapped in a long sweater that had once been yours. The memory of Mom saying, 'She's dead,' the slap-slap of her hands, the *well-that's-done* tone she'd used, rose to the surface whenever I woke. So, I'd turn over and sink back to sleep rather than think about the fact that you were gone for good this time, or that Mom had seemed almost relieved.

When she saw on the calendar that I had plans to attend a party with friends from high school over the weekend, Mom encouraged me to go.

"It'll be good for you to get out," she said.

I wasn't a drinker, but that Saturday night I found myself squeezed into the front seat of a parked car with my friends Mike and Rena, accepting swigs from a bottle of blackberry brandy. It tasted thick and sweet like cough syrup, and I took bigger and bigger gulps whenever it was handed to me. When Mike and Rena started kissing, I stumbled out of the car toward the house, which had grown wavy, as though I was looking at it on a television with bad reception.

Inside, I asked everyone I tripped over in the crowded rooms, "What happened to my sister? Where'd my sister go?"

It was what I wanted them to ask me, though I knew no one would. I hadn't told anyone there what had happened. Since you were never around during my high school years, these friends barely knew I had a sister.

"Where's my sister?" I lurched into the kitchen to ask.

"I don't know. Where?" someone responded like I was offering a riddle.

I tried to make out his blurry face, but the effort gave me a headache.

"Ya know..." I started, then threw up on the table.

Someone helped me to the bathroom so I could finger-brush my teeth. Afterwards, I wandered into the den where I found my friend Ira lounging in a big soft chair. I sat on his lap, looking for trouble.

"Seems you've had a little too much of something," he said, and got up to drive me home.

"Drink lots of water," he told me while I sat slumped beside him in the car, smelling of brandy and peppermint-covered puke. "That way, you won't have a hangover in the morning. Lots of water. Remember."

"What will I tell my mother?" I moaned.

"Tell her you're thirsty," he said, which, at the moment, struck me as incredibly funny.

The following evening, Mom and I had dinner upstairs with Sylvia, who, all these years after the accident, I still thought of as Lisa's mom.

"How about some wine?" she offered.

When I turned green, Mom patted my hand. "Ona's a little under the weather tonight."

I'd admitted to her that I'd had too much to drink and gotten sick at the party, but I didn't tell her about the question I'd thrust at everyone. It never went well when we tried to talk about you. Like me, she never brought up Ray or the baby. When I mentioned you, she remained cool and matter-of-fact. "A social worker told us years ago that, with the way she lived her life, she wouldn't make it to thirty."

"Don't you care?" I'd yell, the echo of *she's dead, slap-slap* with me as I escaped to my room in tears. But Angie, the truth was, I didn't feel grief-stricken either and I hated myself for it. All I felt was numb.

When Kay called, which she did every few days to see how I was holding up, I heard the woodenness in my voice.

"It's heartbreaking, what happened. But, you know, I'm used to being without her."

At least when I was angry at Mom, I felt something.

Dad called often too, from Uncle Manny's in Florida.

"Poor kid," he said. "She was just getting her life together." But mostly, we just shared updates. "Have the detectives called again,

O.?"

"Yesterday. One of them asked me if I knew that there was drug money involved."

"What'd you tell him?"

"That I hadn't known, but that I guess it didn't surprise me."

"I just hope they get the bastard."

"I know," I said. But really, I felt numb about that too.

When Inspector Hendrix or Inspector Sanders called, I dutifully answered their questions. How long was I in San Francisco? When exactly did Ray stop answering the phone? Had I met any of your friends?

I mentioned Greg, though I didn't know his last name, and described the couple who were staying with you, though their names were completely lost to me. When the inspectors pressed for more specifics, I told them I needed to ask my friend who was better at remembering details.

"They want to know what color Ray's parrot was," I said to Kay on the phone one evening.

"He was green, Ona. They kept him in a long thin cage that hung between the kitchen and the living room."

The summer before, when Kay and I were getting to know each other in Boulder, she wrote a poem about me with the line, *Your insides cover your eyes like hair.*

I both loved and hated that line for how accurately it portrayed me. Though I wanted to be observant like Kay, like I knew a writer should be, I tended to moon around, obsessing over my crushes and my insecurities. The tree behind the Boulder Library held little apricots, but I didn't notice them until the young man who occupied my mind that summer climbed its branches, when he saw that I couldn't, and picked them for me. I hardly took in the ruggedly beautiful backdrop of the Flatirons as I window-shopped on Pearl Street for the right dress for a party where that young man would be.

Your insides cover your eyes like hair.

It would be years before I realized that you weren't the only one who dealt with the cruel imbalances in our family by leaving. I ran away too, only I learned to do it without exiting the room.

With Kay's help, I continued to answer the inspectors' questions. But even as I did, I never thought much about who these men were or how hard they were working for us. To me, solving the crime seemed beside the point. Whether or not we found out who did it, you, Ray, and little Ray-Ray would still be dead.

The inspectors filled me in on the fact that you'd been strangled and the baby most likely smothered. They explained that whoever did it had carefully wrapped your three bodies and hid them in a crawlspace beneath the apartment house. Ray's had lain close to the front, so he was easier to spot. It was another three weeks before someone noticed you and Ray-Ray tucked behind a headboard ten feet further back. When I learned this, I thought about the cats of our childhood, the ones Mom had assured us would go under the house in the rain. The ones that never again came home.

To my understanding, Inspectors Hendrix and Sanders cracked the case by following a trail of items the Hendersons stole from you and Ray and sold. Your ring, Ray's parrot, his panel truck, and, finally, the rifle they'd used to kill him.

Decades later, I'd read that Napoleon Hendrix solved close to five hundred homicides over his long career, all while wearing his signature Armani suits, Stetson hat, and snakeskin boots. Upon his retirement in 1999, he told reporters, "When I go to the widow, or the mom, or the kids and say: 'I found the guy who killed your loved one. He's in jail right now - charged with murder,' it's a priceless moment. The look in their eyes right then makes me the richest guy in the world."

I wish I could say that I added to Inspector Hendrix's riches in that way. That I listened, rapt, while he described all he went through to piece together what had happened to the three of you after I left you on that January night. I wish I had said much more to him than perfunctory thank yous. "Thank you for calling… Thank you for letting me know." But that was all I could manage at the time.

When I learned it was the Hendersons who had killed you, I felt blank. If I let myself care who was responsible for your deaths, I'd have to think about what those last moments were like for each of you and I couldn't bring my mind there. Instead, I turned Ray-Ray, with his pudgy legs and goofy grin, into as flimsy a paper doll as I'd made his father, and focused on the one piece of the story I already knew how to grieve. You, the big sister I adored, were gone. Again.

Meanwhile, in a certain way, you were with me more than you'd been in a very long time. Almost every night, you came to me while I waited for sleep. A playful smirk on your lips as you poked at my ribs, saying, "I'm just playing with you," or sang close to my ear, "Stuck in the Middle with You." You let me hold you the way I did the night of Lisa's death. "We were *this* close," you whispered, holding up two crossed fingers. But this time, the other half of *we* was me.

Chapter Eight

I was still in first grade, which means you were still only twelve, when Mom and Dad started talking about sending you away.

"There are special schools for girls who keep looking for trouble."

I don't know if you believed them at first, but I assumed they just said it to scare you. It didn't make any sense. Why banish someone whose worst offense was leaving?

But then, one raw disorienting morning, it was happening.

"When you come home from school this afternoon, Andra's not going to be here," Mom reminded me as I sat at the dinette table poking at my cereal.

Were you gone already? Our goodbye, these many years later, is lost to me. "Be good. Okay, baby?" I can almost hear you say.

That day, I felt sealed off by sadness while the kids in my class busied themselves around me. At the same time, a part of me watched myself go through it. I practiced talking in a monotone and kept my eyes toward the floor, hoping someone would ask what was bothering me. At three o'clock, I walked home slowly, in no hurry to start my new life as an almost-only child.

But when I pushed the door open, you were in the kitchen, crouched in front of the low drawer where we kept the Lorna Dunes and Oreos.

I threw myself on your curled back, wrapping my arms tightly around your neck. "You're here! How come you're here?"

You shrugged. "It was just a warning."

So that's how it works, I thought, feeling like I'd clicked in the last bit of sky in a thousand-piece puzzle.

A few weeks later, Mom said it again. "Remember, when you get home, Andra won't be here." This time, I knew not to believe her.

I spent the afternoon chatting with friends and raising my hand every time the teacher asked the class a question. When the bell rang, I rushed home, certain you'd be there like last time.

"Where is she?" I asked when I found Mom alone in the kitchen.

"Oh, honey, you know. We told you."

I went to our room, pulled your flannel shirt off your desk chair, and wrapped myself in it. It smelled like you, just as it had when I wore it on Halloween to be a hobo. You had dressed as a hippie in your bell-bottoms and love beads so not everyone could tell it was a costume. While we trick-or-treated, you saw a boy you knew from school and quickly made me hold your treat bag against mine so it looked like there was only one.

"I have to take my little sister trick-or-treating," you told the boy, rolling your eyes. But after we passed him, you gave me a wink, letting me know that was the trick. The treat was being with me.

Now you were gone again. But this time, you hadn't run away. They made you go. "They turned you against me, didn't they?" I worried that you'd been right. If I'd gotten sad like last time, you probably wouldn't have been sent anywhere.

Over the next year, you were gone so often, I lost track of whether you'd run off again or been sent away. You were home, gone, home again. A jump rope swinging skyward, then slapping the pavement with no discernable rhythm.

It was during this unpredictable time that you brought home a puppy and convinced Mom and Dad to let us keep her. Like with the kittens, Mom wouldn't let us bring Sammy into the house, so she slept on the front porch in a doghouse Dad made from an old hollowed out television.

Not long after we got her, you were sent somewhere new, a girls' boarding school in Hudson, New York. I'd never seen anywhere you'd lived away from home and, when I tried to imagine this place, I pictured a line of teenagers standing frozen in a row like Barbies at the toy store.

I thought maybe if Sammy could sleep at the foot of my bed, my room wouldn't feel so empty at night. I mentioned this to Mom, but you can probably guess what she said. "I'm not spending my life vacuuming up dog hair."

Afraid Sammy might pull me down, Mom and Dad wouldn't let me walk her. They were the ones who fed Sammy and took her out.

"She's a good dog," they'd say, but I don't recall them petting Sammy all that much or talking sweetly to her. I'd show her short bursts of affection, but soon I'd grow bored and run off to play with friends or slam into the house where my toys were.

Outside in her hollow TV, Sammy accepted my random bouts of interest in her. You were the one who was good with animals. Still, I didn't think of Sammy as yours. Instead, I had a vague sense that she was like you, adopted into our family, but not completely.

Do you remember we came that summer to the upstate boarding school for your fourteenth birthday? It surprised me that the campus was so pretty. As we sat together at a picnic table, surrounded by trees and far off mountains, you must have told us something about your days there. But your words are as lost to me as the dialogue on the silent screen at the drive-in across from the motel where we'd stayed the night before. All I recall is needing to touch you. I smoothed your hair back from your face until you asked me to stop. "It's just that it's a little annoying."

A while later, the two of us strolled around the grounds and you proudly introduced me to the people we passed. "This is *my* little sister!"

In the bathroom, we ran into a girl you knew by the sinks, and she studied us in the mirror. "Yup. I can see you're sisters."

We grinned at each other, silently agreeing not to mention that we weren't blood-related. I loved when people commented on our resemblance, even if it was just our brown eyes and chestnut hair that were similar.

We came there one more time that summer, but all I remember from that second visit is the hole in your smile. At home you'd worn braces, and then a retainer you'd take out to speak to boys and had eventually lost. One front tooth never quite straightened and now it was gone.

"That witch of a dentist insisted on pulling it," you told us, holding back tears. "She ordered a bridge for me. But, meanwhile, I have to go around looking like this."

What I didn't say, as Dad griped about how much he'd spent trying to fix that tooth, was that I understood how you felt from the inside out. Earlier that same summer, Holly, the meanest girl on our block, chose a day when we were the only two to be sent out to play to suggest that we "walk like people who limp." Something about the game made me uneasy, but we had nothing else to do. When she started hobbling in a circle, I followed, doing my best to imitate her awkward moves.

"Just walk like you always do," Holly said, stopping to observe me. "You walk like people who limp."

That's when I got it. I may have only had to wear my leg brace at night, but my cerebral palsy wasn't a secret like I'd always thought.

I watched Holly drag one foot behind her, and had to work not to cry, knowing that all day, every day, I went around looking like that.

While you were still in Hudson with the tooth thief and a school full of teenage girls who couldn't live at home either, Mom, Dad, and I watched a made-for-television movie called *Maybe I'll Come Home in the Spring*. In it, Sally Field plays a teenage runaway who has decided to hitchhike home. I sat on the couch mesmerized as the Flying Nun with long hippie hair and dirty jeans walked precariously through traffic, the sound of honking cars interrupted by a voice that could have been yours.

In a flashback phone call to her parents, Sally Field as Dennie asked if they hated her.

I glanced at Mom and Dad. "I was afraid this number wouldn't work," I'd heard you tell them when I picked up the extension. "You wouldn't change the locks, would you?" That was back when you'd call from a payphone on the street. Now, at your boarding school, you weren't allowed to call us at all.

After that night, *Maybe I'll Come Home in the Spring* showed up frequently on the 4:30 Movie. I watched it every time. Dennie had a younger sister, but Susie was nothing like me. She was a teenager who kept a drug stash in the medicine cabinet and was thinking of running away herself. Toward the end of the movie, she told Dennie she felt mad at her for coming home. Whenever I watched it, those words stunned me. Andra knows I want her home, I assured myself. She knows.

Throughout the movie, Dennie kept asking her parents if she could stay.

"Of course," they answered. And she did, she stayed, which is why I watched it over and over. As the credits rolled, Dennie was always right there, running the vacuum in her family's living room.

Chapter Nine

The first summer after your death, I went back to Boulder where I roomed with Kay again and took more classes at Naropa. The school was celebrating the twenty-fifth anniversary of Jack Kerouac's *On the Road*, and famous writers and radicals kept coming through town to take part in panel discussions or teach workshops. William Burroughs, Abbie Hoffman, Robert Creeley. Most everyone around me was star-struck, but I only had a CliffsNotes understanding of who these people were. I'd started *On the Road* and, though I saw the beauty in its momentum, I couldn't read it with the fervor in which it was written. I could barely stay still long enough to complete a page.

We had a friend that summer, Kurt, who was handsome, friendly, and very full of himself. He liked to brag that he'd slept with five hundred women.

"Do you think it's true?" I asked Kay one morning as we sat on the floor of our terrace, sharing a plate of scrambled eggs.

"That's one woman a day for almost a year and a half. I think he might be exaggerating."

The evening before, as we walked home from a reading at the school, Kurt had pulled up beside us on a motorcycle, revving the engine on an otherwise quiet road.

"Just got this beauty. Who'd like to hop on?"

I thought of the ride I almost took with Greg and his friends from the Hell's Angels on what would have been a futile search for you and Ray.

"You mind?" I asked Kay.

I was dressed ridiculously wrong for a motorcycle ride in my nearly sheer cotton summer dress. But, as I bunched up the skirt and climbed on, Kurt's only warning as he passed me a helmet was, "Careful not to let your leg touch the pipe."

We flew through town and headed toward the mountains, the cool twilit air turning to wind and the road rushing beneath us. Too soon, we were in the hills and Kurt stopped the bike. Forgetting about the hot pipe, I slid down, burning my leg.

"You're going to have a nice scar there," he said.

We sat in the grass and passed a canteen of water between us. The mark on my calf throbbed. But it wasn't as bad as it might have been, since it was on my numb right side. For a moment, a flicker, I pictured the glint in your eyes when I showed you the scar. "That's a badge of honor, baby," I imagined you'd say.

Instead of dropping me at home, Kurt parked by his own apartment. Without a word, I followed him upstairs where I spent the night.

"We did everything but," I told Kay now as we ate our eggs.

"Sounds like good Catholic girl sex," she teased.

"Thank you, Mary Kathryn. Does that make me a bad Jewish girl?"

I didn't actually like Kurt, nor did I think he especially liked me. There was a guy named David I was genuinely interested in. A lanky musician I'd shared a few shy kisses with at a party. David didn't have a car, and when his much older friend, a math professor, offered to drive me home from the gathering, I took the ride. For no other reason than the suggestive way he touched my knee, I made out passionately with the professor in his front seat that night, his fingers finding their way inside me. Not even Kay knew about that. I hadn't told anyone.

Wild child and earnest student. Promiscuous virgin. You had been the bad girl while I was the good. Being a combination of both was the one way I could figure out to keep you with me. Not that I understood that at the time. I believed I was collecting experience, for my writing, for the adventure. I believed I was just being nineteen.

On the morning of what would have been your twenty-sixth birthday, I sat out on the terrace and worked on a poem for you. We had an assignment from the poet Anne Waldman to write a piece in which every line began with the phrase *I remember*, so I used that form.

> *I remember that you loved Elvis movies and celery*
> *with cream cheese and the smell of gas stations.*
> *Mostly I remember that you loved music.*
>
> *I remember you singing "My Baby Loves Lovin'"*
> *and "Build Me Up Buttercup," and dancing to*
> *"(I'm Not Your) Steppin' Stone" on the bed across*
> *the room from mine...*

I filled three pages with memories of you, my vibrant older sister who teased, poked, and protected me, and broke my heart when she ran away. I wrote how you'd always been leaving and now you were gone. Anyone reading it would think you'd run away one last time and I'd simply lost track of you.

For the few weeks I was home that summer, I was surly and curt with Mom and Dad. Sadness pulsed deep within me and, unable to let it rise to the surface, I just felt mean. When I finally returned to Purchase, I signed up to see a therapist on campus. In our first couple of sessions, I used my allotted forty-five minutes to discuss classes, tangles with roommates, and my wish for a boyfriend. Finally, I mentioned, as off-handedly as I could, that my sister had been murdered.

"Oh! I'm so sorry," the therapist said, leaning forward in her chair. "You must be devastated."

"I don't think about it much," I admitted.

Squirming, I recalled a winter night, freshman year, when I'd left the library in tears after learning of a different murder. Friends of mine, anticipating how upset I'd be, met me in the quad and held me while I sobbed.

"To be honest, I took it harder when John Lennon was killed." There, I thought. Now she understands what a gaping hole I have in place of a heart.

But the therapist simply shrugged. "That's what celebrities are for."

As I headed back to my dorm, I felt better than I had in months. Makes sense, I decided. Celebrities give us a safe place to put our feelings. For what was now almost a year, I had been walking around hating myself for continuing on with my life as though you hadn't been violently ripped out of it. But if this therapist was right, I wasn't an unfeeling person. It was a sign of health that I could function so well. Still, as our sessions continued, I expected her to encourage me to talk about you and the devastating way your life ended. Each week that she didn't bring it up, I felt both disappointed and relieved.

After I graduated Purchase, I moved to Brooklyn and, like Mom, took a job as a receptionist at a local real estate office. What felt different about this place in Park Slope was that all the rental and sales agents were really something else. A drummer, a photographer, a chef. So, it seemed, I fit right in. The poet who answered their phones.

The following year, I entered the master's program in poetry at NYU and volunteered at Goldwater, a chronic care hospital on Roosevelt Island where the poet Sharon Olds ran workshops for the patients. I took dictation for her students whose physical limitations prevented them from writing or typing on their own. Each week, I began my visit with Marie who, paralyzed from the neck down, composed poems aloud in her breathy voice. Next, I'd assist Julia who, for sixteen years, had lain in a back ward where she was thought to be brain dead. Somehow, someone finally discovered that, though she could neither move her body nor speak, Julia could communicate by lifting her eyes. Her intelligence was very much alive.

Though I originally volunteered at Goldwater to meet Sharon Olds and learn from her, I soon found my own connection to the patients. The hospital reminded me of United Cerebral Palsy. Angie, do you remember our monthly drives to that sprawling health center for my physical therapy appointments? I hated the place, with its smell of saliva and dust, and the kids we saw in the halls and waiting rooms whose bodies jerked and shook in their wheelchairs. Embarrassed and ashamed, I believed those other kids were somehow truer versions of me.

It felt different now. I admired the patients I met at Goldwater. Each had survived the unsurvivable and had a rich, tenacious inner life. In the writing workshop, they spoke openly about the accidents and mysterious illnesses that brought them there. Unlike them, I had no idea how to talk about the trauma I'd lived through. Though, of course it was there, like an inflammation just beneath my skin. I still rarely discussed it with friends and, to be honest, I don't remember thinking about it that often. Yet when I look at the poems I wrote that year, I'm struck by how many are about you.

I wrote how I'd felt abandoned by you as a child:

She was always leaving. / Those mornings, waking,

/ it seemed the house had grown unwanted rooms...

I attempted to paint your portrait with words:

*You could be beside me at this mirror / the way I
have your body memorized, / mole at the ankle,
pink-white marbly skin. / Cigarette smoke staying
in your hair for a halo...*

At my most courageous, I expressed how guilty I felt:

*Andra, the truth is I wished it.
Not the death that hit you
sudden as a chunk of ice,
but this catching up,
this waking up
and finding myself your age...*

But while you were my most faithful muse, I didn't give a single line to Ray or the baby. In the drafts I brought to my classes, no one had been strangled, smothered, or shot. One young woman, a beloved sister, had died, inexplicably.

"Pain engraves a deeper memory." The quote—I looked it up—comes from the poet, Anne Sexton. She's right, of course. Pain, like a hot tattoo needle, makes certain moments indelible. But shame? Shame is an eraser.

I had a boyfriend at the time who wanted to squeeze my neck during sex the way he had with a previous lover. "It makes orgasms really intense," he promised, but I refused, having heard how dangerous this was. Twice, he brought his fingers to my throat, hoping I'd changed my mind. I pushed them away and, afterwards, found myself flinching every time he so much as grazed my collarbone.

You had been choked to death, but not once in the months I dated that rough boy, nor for years afterward, did the correlation cross my mind.

Before the school year ended, that boyfriend and I had broken up. I felt adrift until a friend in Brooklyn told me about a summer sublet he knew of in Berkeley, California.

"New York is sticky and smelly in the summer," I said, considering. What I didn't say was that this could be a kind of pilgrimage for me. A pilgrimage in search of my grief.

When I landed at SFO, it seemed the trip was charmed. Though I called for an ordinary taxi to take me to Berkeley, the only car available was a stretch limo with smoked windows.

"I can't pay for this," I told the driver after he explained that the car was meant for actor/director Ron Howard, who'd had a change in plans.

"You called for a cab, you'll pay for a cab," he said, holding the door open while I slid onto the wide, plush seat. As we crossed the Bay Bridge, I let myself imagine that you had arranged this lavish welcome from the beyond.

There were a few other charmed moments that summer. A day trip with my housemates to Napa Valley, a Holly Near concert on campus where I ran into a high school friend. But most afternoons, I took the BART into San Francisco alone. As I roamed your chosen hometown, I missed you terribly. But I'd spent so much of my life missing you, the feeling was simply familiar.

Unable to mourn, I worked to shape my fruitless wanderings into poems.

> *In Manhattan your absence*
> *is normal like thick heat in August,*
> *the facts behind it, words, an idea.*
> *My sister who lives in San Francisco is dead.*

So, in your city I figure I'll meet up with it
in every Victorian doorway,
or breathe it in with the fajitas
in the Mission District air.
But even the heat evades me here.
I'm all chicken skin and shivers
as I wander up streets so steep
they make a horizon I can't see behind,
and the fog hovers like a perfect ghost
but isn't you.

A Giant's game, a day on the Santa Cruz boardwalk riding the kiddy rides. I just caught myself almost describing these excursions with my housemates as breathers for me. But before the word makes it to the page, its more literal meaning surfaces. *Breather.* One who breathes. Either Philip or Velma Henderson had pressed the breath out of you. I am a breather, and you once were. I am a breather, and you are ash.

As it happened, that summer, 1986, the Hendersons were finally sentenced. The morning of their hearing, I entered the San Francisco Hall of Justice wearing black cotton Mary Janes. When the guard waved his metal detecting rod near my feet, the tiny buckles beeped. He grinned and waved me through.

I slid onto a hard bench at the back of the courtroom and listened while several people were given their sentences for smaller crimes. A robbery. An assault. After what felt like a long time, the Hendersons were brought in. There, a mere few feet away, was the same ill-matched couple I remembered. Philip: tattooed, slim, and handsome. Velma: weathered and harsh-looking but for her long shiny hair. I studied the Hendersons, neither of whom ever looked my way, trying to see the thing inside them that would let them kill a young pregnant woman, a sweet bear of a man, an infant.

Monsters, I thought. But they appeared ordinary in their prison suits that fit like kid's pajamas. Velma even wore a plastic baby barrette in her hair.

The two of them stood, hands cuffed behind their backs, calmly awaiting their fates. Finally, the judge spoke.

"For the murder of Raymond Martin Boggs II. For the murder of Andrea Gritz Boggs. For the murder of Raymond Martin Boggs III..."

At that litany of names, a single sob erupted from inside me. Other families have funerals and we have this, I thought, wiping my wet face with the one torn tissue I could find.

As I was leaving the courtroom, I met Ray's mother. "Angie was my sister," I told her, according to a poem I wrote that afternoon. But the truth is, I don't remember Mrs. Boggs or anything about our encounter. This, I'm thinking, was the start of my amnesia.

Facts—spare, generalized—stayed with me, but the details left. You began to exist for me only in scattered, half-remembered vignettes from our childhood. When I talked about you, it was in a single, practiced sentence. "I had an older sister I worshipped growing up." If I went a bit deeper with a close friend or a man I'd made myself vulnerable to, I described the loneliness and abandonment issues I'd carried from the time you began leaving home. As for how you died, and who died with you, that was a tale I shared only when I had to. Inside me, it dulled to a faded newspaper account.

As she combs her hair, does she remember yours?
Mix of shampoo and smoke,
light hitting the light brown making it blond.
Does he ever picture his hands on your throat,
shooting Ray,
pressing the breath out of the baby
until that little boy was still as a stone?

Do they undo it in dreams,
taking up each body,
limp and beautiful as Jesus in the Pieta,
to cradle, to kiss,
to breathe the life back in?

Other families have funerals and we have this, I put in that poem. Yet I never thought to ask our parents why we hadn't held a memorial for the three of you. Nor did I ask myself why, at nineteen, I hadn't insisted on it or held one of my own. It occurs to me now that when I went back to my Berkeley sublet after the sentencing and started to work on a poem, I was crafting a kind of cabinet. A neat place to store the little bit I'd let myself feel that day. That's fine. It's one of the functions of art. But the cabinet drawers had locks and I kept them sealed for years. More years, Angie, than you had lived.

Chapter Ten

As I write this, I'm fifty-eight, which means I've lived without you for nearly four decades. Our parents are long gone. Our once secret half-siblings too. I'm married to my second husband, Dan, and I have a son. Ethan is twenty-four now, the age I turned a month after the Hendersons' sentencing, the age you were the last time you lived a full year.

About a decade ago, a succession of small events began to bring you back to me. A picture of you showed up for just a moment in a slideshow at our half-brother Steve's memorial, and it hit me that, as the sole survivor of our immediate family, I was the only person in that crowded room of mourners who knew who you were. Some weeks later, "My Baby Loves Lovin'" came on the radio and, though I'd heard it countless times through the years, my eyes filled at the thought that I alone remembered how you loved that song. Then Ethan—thirteen and angry that I wouldn't let him buy a particular video game—threatened to run away, and while the rational side of me knew he didn't mean it, an ancient and familiar panic rose in me like steam.

Not long after that, my earlobe tore, as yours once had, and my own reaction to that little injury startled me awake.

"Weird," my husband murmured as he fingered the split skin. Dan is also a poet, and we were standing in a subway station after giving a reading together in a crowded New York pub. "I've never seen anything like this."

"Oh, I have," I said tightly, picturing not just your stretched, elongated lobe, but your missing front tooth, your tattooed lower belly, and the cigarette burning to ash between your fingers. This doesn't happen to people like me, I thought, clutching my tasteful little earring. I'm not like her. Finally, hearing the disdain I never knew I felt, I recognized Mom's voice.

I adored my sister, I did, I told myself as I lay on the table in a plastic surgeon's office having my earlobe mended. I adored Angie, I repeated in the days that followed. The words became a kind of mantra, but what I mostly heard in my head was your hurt, angry voice as you knelt on my bed in our childhood room. "They turned you against me, didn't they?" "No," I'd cried at the time, horrified. I never wanted to be set against you, but of course I'd been. Of course, as much as I loved you, I also internalized Mom's hypercritical view of you and, along with it, her belief that I was somehow more worthy.

I lived in Hoboken, New Jersey, then, just across the river from Manhattan. One drizzly weekday afternoon, off from work at our local library, I pulled a plastic bin of curled family photos from the back of my closet and sat on the floor browsing through them. In my favorite picture of you and me together, we're seated at a picnic table. Your hair is styled in a *That Girl* flip. Your bare arms, full and lovely, frame my head as I rest against you, eyes closed in a kind of little sister love doze.

Penciled on the back, *Hudson 1970*, in Dad's blocky print. Decades had passed since I last thought of our trips to the boarding school with its sprawling grounds and distant mountains. Those visits gave me my first glimpse of your life apart from us, but I didn't really know anything about the place. As I stared at our young faces, I realized that, at nearly twice the age you ever got to be, I had no more understanding of your life than I'd had as a seven-year-old girl wandering with you around campus.

I laid the photo aside and began to reach for another, but something pulled at me. Couldn't I, if I chose to, learn more?

Ethan came home then, bursting through the door, hungry for an afterschool snack. As we sat at the table, he described how his humanities teacher had given the class busywork so she could use the period to answer her email.

"She told me I didn't spend enough time on this," he said, taking a sheet of paper from his backpack. "But I'm pretty sure she just wanted me to keep messing with it so she wouldn't have to figure out something else for me to do."

I talked to him and read through his work, but all the while I thought about you, sent to that boarding school in Hudson at the very age he was then.

By the time Ethan finished his snack, the rain had stopped. He answered a text, got another, and then left, as abruptly as he'd arrived, to meet friends by the pier.

Alone again, I opened my laptop and found the number for the public library in Hudson, New York. I'd been a librarian for nearly fifteen years by then, but not once had it occurred to me to use my research skills on your behalf. My heart beat hard as I picked up the phone. I couldn't shake the feeling that I was somehow trespassing as I took this step toward the past.

"Reference," a woman's voice chimed.

"Um, hi. I have a question I hope you can answer. My sister attended a boarding school in your town in 1970. Would you know what the name of it might've been?"

"It could be one of two places," the librarian told me. "Including right here. This used to be an orphanage and, back then, parents sometimes sent their troubled kids here."

I glanced at the photo now propped on my desk. A lawn stretched and filled the frame.

"My sister's school had a large, grassy campus. There were picnic tables..."

"That was probably the New York State Training School for Girls. It's a men's prison now, but back then it was a girls' reformatory."

"A reformatory," I repeated. Of course.

"Were there red brick buildings?" the librarian asked.

"I don't remember."

"If there were, it was the Training School."

When we hung up, I returned to the photo bin. In another picture marked *Hudson*, you stand in a white miniskirt, smiling at the camera while I kneel in the grass between your parted legs. Behind us is a brick building. Under the beating sun, it's faded to pink.

With just a few keystrokes, I had two articles about the Training School by a journalist named Nina Bernstein. I printed them out and sank onto the couch, aware that reading them would take me to the other side of something I'd come to count on. A vagueness that had allowed me to let you go.

Chapter Eleven

When you finally came home from your year in Hudson, you looked beautiful with new blond streaks in your hair, tight bell bottom jeans, and high wedge shoes. I remember you had to go to Phoenix House for counseling and that, one afternoon, you brought me with you.

It seemed like an ordinary house, but bigger and pushed back from the street.

"This used to be some kind of hotel," you explained.

Inside, we joined a circle of teenagers who sat cross-legged on the floor, talking about their feelings.

"My folks blame me for everything," you told them. "Nothing I do is ever good enough for my mother."

It made me feel bad to hear your voice shake and see your eyes grow wet, ruining your mascara. I rested my hand on your knee, but gazed around the room, letting my mind drift away from your sadness. Across from me sat a beautiful girl with a pearl on the side of her nose I couldn't stop staring at. It looked like a dab of cream filling.

That afternoon, our parents met us at Phoenix House for a family session. Mom brought books for me to look at in the waiting room, but when the counselor poked his head through the door, he suggested I come too.

"She's just impossible," Mom complained to the counselor. "She steals from us. She smokes. Grown men call the house asking for her. God knows what she does when she's off on her own."

I let my mind wander back to the girl with the pearl on her nose. She probably glued it there, I decided. It stayed in place so perfectly. Days before, I'd glued my eyes shut, trying to put on your false eyelashes. This must be how people go blind, I thought in a panic. But when I groped my way out of the bathroom, you led me back in and lightly patted the glue away with a wet cotton ball.

"Oh, Ona." You laughed, but not in a way that made me feel stupid for what I had done. It was a tender chuckle I found comforting. I couldn't understand why Mom never noticed your gentle side. Recently, I'd tried to describe the difference between how she treated the two of us in a composition about fairness for school. I wrote that Mom often yelled at and punished you, but was overly nice to me. For an example of that niceness, I told how, the year before, I'd gotten in trouble in school and had to write *I Must Not Talk in Class* fifty times for homework. Halfway through, Mom felt bad for me and took over. "Why would she do that?" my teacher asked in red. Teachers always loved my compositions, but on the back of the page, instead of a compliment, Mrs. Reiss wrote, "None of this makes sense. Explain." I flushed the color of her angry pencil and smashed the paper down to the bottom of my book bag, embarrassed and mad at myself for trying to describe something I didn't have words for.

Now, jiggling your crossed leg, you told the counselor, "My dad won't let me hug him anymore."

Dad shifted in his chair. "It makes me uncomfortable. The way she presses her body against me."

The counselor nodded, and I wondered if there was something wrong in the way you hugged Dad. Did you want him to notice your breasts and hips?

I flashed back to your thirteenth birthday, nearly two years before. "Hey, you're a teenager now!" I'd pointed out. But you said,

"You're not a real teenager until you're fourteen." That seemed wrong so I asked Natalie, whose sister was even older than you. "Of course thirteen's a teenager," she told me. "Listen. Thir-*teen*." At the time, I couldn't understand how you didn't know that. But now, maybe I did. As grown as you were, a part of you still wanted to be a girl, able to hug your daddy.

The people at Phoenix House encouraged family vacations, so that summer we went to Deer Park Lodge in the Catskills. Remember the paneled basement where you and I headed each morning after breakfast, our pockets heavy with coins? You'd put yours in the pinball machine while I spent mine in the jukebox, playing "Knock Three Times," "Joy to the World," and "Let It Be." When my favorites were over, you and your friends made requests. I knew you were all avoiding spending your pinball money in the jukebox, but I didn't mind. The kids my age were outside playing sports that my cerebral palsy would make me mess up, so I was happy to play D.J. for the teenagers.

"Let's hear 'Bobbie McGee,' kiddo," Kyle, a cute boy with long hair, said.

While I pressed the jukebox buttons, Kyle leaned into the pinball machine, and you rested a hand on his back.

"Is Kyle your boyfriend?" I asked that night as we got ready for bed in our cabin.

You studied yourself in the dresser mirror. "I'm working on it."

Before meals, a xylophone chimed over the loudspeaker like an announcement at school. "Dinner is now being served in the children's dining hall."

One evening, you didn't show up to eat at the teen table. I thought maybe you were off somewhere with Kyle, but then he and another boy came in, jostling loudly.

Dragging the food around on my plate, I watched the door. Finally, I wandered to the lobby and waited as the crickets sang their you're-in-the-country song through the open windows. After what felt like forever, you finally burst in and plopped down beside me.

"Where were you?"

Your cheeks were flushed, your hair falling loose from its rubber band.

"The scariest thing happened. I was taking a walk and some guy followed me. I was almost raped."

"What's *raped*?" All I could think was how much the word sounded like *grape*.

"Shush! Lower your voice. Some guy I don't know tried to have sex with me."

"How can someone you don't know have sex with you?"

You sighed and rolled your eyes. "You're no help."

Spotting one of your girlfriends, you walked off. I watched the two of you lean against the cigarette machine and whisper to each other, the words *grape, rape, grape* sing-songing through my head.

A few months later, after running away again, you were placed in a foster home. I remember the kids who lived there with you, a slim quiet girl of fourteen and a four-year-old with beautiful blond curls. On our first visit, I took the little one outside to play in the yard. She picked up a twig and pretended to smoke it.

"Cigarettes are bad for you," I told her.

She looked surprised. Everyone in that house smoked. The foster parents, you, even the shy girl.

On the drive home, Mom told Dad that she didn't like how your foster mother had been asleep on the couch when we got there.

"I'm guessing she's a shikker," she said, the Yiddish word for *drunk*.

How many families did you need? I wondered. You had us, and a birth family somewhere, and now a foster family where everyone did the kinds of things you got in trouble for. Did our parents really think their home was better for you than ours? Was the shy girl a better sister because you were closer in age? Probably, I thought, remembering you saying, "You're no help" the night of the almost-rape in the country.

Meanwhile, the pretty little blond girl got to have dinner with you every night while I ate with an *I Love Lucy* rerun for company.

Chapter Twelve

A few days after I made that long overdue call to the Hudson Library and filled in that one piece of your past, I phoned our old grade school, P.S. 104.

"How long do you keep student records?" I asked the woman who answered the phone.

"We give them to the next school, and then they pass them on from there. Where did you go to high school?"

I explained that the information I sought was about my deceased sister, and that you'd never made it past eighth grade.

"Where did she go to middle school?"

I was at a loss. My school, I.S. 53, had been merely a year old when I started. Five years earlier, you took a bus to junior high in another part of Rockaway. Did I ever know its name?

"Hold on a sec," the woman said. "Let me just check one thing."

While I waited, a number popped into my head. *180.* What was that? Why was I thinking of it now?

"Andrea Gritz, right?" the woman asked, coming back on the line. "And you must be Ona. I'm holding two handwritten index cards. You came here for kindergarten and Andrea came in third grade."

"That's right." We existed, I thought, as though I'd been waiting for such proof.

"I'm afraid that's all I've got," she said, sounding genuinely sorry. "Is there anything else I can help you with?"

"Actually, yes. Could you tell me... there wasn't a school called

180, was there?"

"There sure was. Junior High School 180 in Rockaway Park. Is that where Andrea went? It's Scholar's Academy now, but they might still have her records."

I hung up certain you had whispered the detail I needed into my ear.

The woman in the records office at Scholar's Academy seemed unsure of me at first.

"We have her records," she said in a guarded tone. "But we'll need a copy of her official death certificate and a notarized letter stating who you are. Now, what do you want this information for?"

"Well," I said, feeling my way toward an answer as I spoke. "I don't have her anymore. Andrea can't describe her life to me. So, I'm trying to piece together what I can."

There was silence on the line, and I wondered if I should have given a more pragmatic response.

"That's touching," she finally said. "We just have to be cautious with so much identity theft going on. And Ona, I'm sorry for your loss."

My eyes began to burn. People had said that to me when our parents passed away, eight years earlier, and more recently when our half-brother Steve died. But I felt quite sure this was the only time anyone, other than Kay when we first found out, ever said it to me about you.

All those years, I had barely allowed you to enter my mind, but now I thought of you constantly. In the weeks it took for your death certificate to arrive in the mail, I spent hours at home staring at your face in photographs, and stolen moments at work typing variations of your name into search boxes online.

On our library's ancestry database, I found a death record for you under Angie Boggs.

"Sex: Female... Birth Date: 26 Jul 1956... Birthplace: New York... Death Date: 19 Mar 1982... Death Place: San Francisco."

I stared at the screen, my throat tightening. You were killed in January, but it fit my memory of the long weeks of worrying about you that your body wouldn't have been discovered until March.

Andrea Susan Gritz, I typed and closed my eyes, willing a birth record to appear. Instead, I saw another death record with the same information as the first. According to the site, you, never having been born, died twice.

Googling epilepsy, I learned of its long history of stigmatization. I read up on Phenobarbital, the medication you had been given to control your seizures, and found that it's linked to hyperactivity and behavioral problems.

On a Name Your Baby website, I searched *Andra*. From the Greek, it means strong, courageous. You had to be, I thought. Next, I typed in *Ona*. Though I'd always known my name to mean oneness or unity, here I found another definition. From the Hebrew: Graced, favored one. I flinched, recalling how, growing up, being so blatantly favored made me feel like the evil stepsister in a fairytale, even as it made me feel secure.

Chapter Thirteen

"Where's your sister?"

The question came up less and less as the sight of me leaving our house alone grew more common. When someone did ask, my answer was always the same. "She's a runaway." *A* runaway. Not, "She ran away," which would be a single action, a verb that could be set in reverse. You were a runaway like you were an epileptic, like you were a sister. Sometimes, you took off, and neither our parents nor I could say where you were. Other times, you were living where they put you—a boarding school or foster home. But even then, you were there because of what you were, a runaway. It was as complete an answer as I knew to give.

You were the late-night phone call I usually slept through. The reason Dad had to rush out of the house in the middle of watching *Columbo*. A missing girl who had surfaced behind a locked door in someone's apartment and refused to come out until she heard her father's voice.

"She's a runaway," I'd say because it was the closest I could come to saying you were an absence. The name on the extra pass I lent to friends so they could come with me to our beach club in summer. The girl whose empty bed those same friends slept in when they spent the night. Yours was the voice on the other end of the line when I least expected it, a voice that often sounded urgent and rushed.

"Is Mom or Dad there? Come on, baby. It's important."

"Are you an only child?"

By the time I was in fifth grade, I heard this question more often than "Where's your sister?"

"No," I'd answer quickly, but I believed the truth was really no and yes. If only children were lonely, which I imagined they were, I was more so since I had someone specific to miss. Worse than that, unlike real only children, I had been left. I was leavable.

For a few months, you lived near us, actually in Far Rockaway, with a family in the Redfern Projects. I had one friend who lived there too—Jody, a quiet boy as small as I was who showed me photos of beautiful places whenever our class went to the school library in the afternoons.

"Do you know my sister? Andra?" I once asked him as we looked at a book about the Grand Canyon. "She's staying in Redfern."

"That's your sister? Everyone knows her. She's the only White person there."

After Redfern, you lived with the guy who worked for Kentucky Fried Chicken in some other part of Queens. "At least she won't go hungry," Dad sighed.

The summer before I started intermediate school, you called to tell me you wanted to be called *Angie*.

"Because of the song?" I asked. "Angie" played on the radio almost every time I turned it on. It was one of my favorites, along with Elton John's "Daniel" about a guy who missed his brother.

"Yup. What do you think? Do you like it on me?"

"Yeah, it's pretty."

What I really thought was that Andra, the girl who had shared my room, would be gone now in a new way. Still, the next afternoon, while Mom and I were in town, I pulled her into a record shop to buy the 45.

"The Sto-nes!" the guy at the counter drawled approvingly.

"The *Rolling* Stones," I corrected him, afraid he might give me the wrong song.

Too soon, September came and, at my new school, I suddenly felt like The Crippled Kid. We had to switch rooms for each class, and it was hard for me to get from one to the next in the five minutes they gave us. Also, since many of us were strangers to each other at I.S. 53, both teachers and kids randomly asked me if I'd hurt my leg. Worst of all, a boy in my homeroom made fun of how I held my right arm, bending his at the elbow, dropping his wrists, and panting at me like a dog.

When I finally got home from those long days, I did what you'd taught me to do, retreat into music and make believe. Alone in what had once been our room, I'd watch my shadowy reflection in the blank TV screen and pretend to be the star of my own show as I sang along to 45's. "Killing Me Softly with His Song." "I Got a Name." When my friend Kerry stayed over, we played that it was still the sixties and we were Beatle wives. Only once in a while, I was just myself, listening to Carly Simon's *No Secrets* album and studying the cover where she looked a little like you with her long dark hair, her elegant hands, the globes of her breasts visible beneath her clingy blue blouse. I'd pull out the lyric sheet and imagine Carly Simon was my sister, sharing confidences, telling stories, and giving advice, all in the words of her songs.

In eighth grade, I had a wonderful English teacher who used song lyrics to get us interested in poetry. That's when I began to fill notebooks with poems and stories, discovering that words can also offer escape.

I think it was the following year, when I started high school, that you went out west. That summer, Mom and I made plans to see you in San Francisco for your twenty-first birthday. As a present, I wrote a poem to put in a handmade card:

> *Not everyone has a sister*
> *who's pretty and sweet and fun.*
> *But I have that kind of sister,*
> *and she's turning twenty-one.*
> *She's out in San Francisco*
> *where the trees are always green*
> *and she's the most loved sister*
> *that city has ever seen.*

The only problem was my sloppy handwriting. Fortunately, Kerry knew calligraphy.

"Your sister is going to love this," she said as she artfully inscribed my words.

How long had it been since we'd last seen you? A year and a half? More? We met up in the lobby of our hotel, and I couldn't help noticing how wrung out you looked. Your long hair had grown dry and brittle, and you were skeleton thin. I kept staring at your forehead, which somehow seemed too big.

Up in our room, Mom took a nap while you and I stretched out on the other bed, talking quietly.

"So, my baby sister's in high school. You like any guys?"

"Kind of," I said, thinking of a boy named Danny who had wild curly hair. He lived in a group home and, when I first visited him there, I wondered why no one had thought of that place, in walking distance from our house, back when they decided you couldn't live at home. I also wondered if Danny had a little sister somewhere missing him. "You get used to it," I'd have assured her if I could.

I told you a bit about him, but I was having trouble paying attention to our conversation. Your gaunt appearance was too distracting. It said something about your life now, but I didn't know what, so I focused on the one fix I could think of. "Since you've lost so much weight and your forehead's so high, you might look better with bangs."

It was when Mom's nap was over that we went downstairs to meet Tina, our hippie distant cousin, my doppelganger, who lived in San Francisco too.

Do you remember what happened right after she got there, and we were all talking out on the street? A friend of hers saw us and came over, and Tina introduced Mom to her as *her* mom. It surprised me, but I figured it must have been a form of shorthand, as though it would have been too much trouble to say, "I want you to meet my father's cousin."

Instead of going out to eat, like I expected, we headed back up to our room to talk. Angie, I never asked how you felt when you first learned the truth about Tina and Steve. But when Mom said, "I have something important to talk to you about," and you dropped next to me on the bed and took my hand, I felt terrified. I could tell that you and Tina already knew what the important something was. You'd all discussed this ahead of time. How I would be told. When.

"Who's sick?" I made myself ask, though I was thinking, which one of us is dying?

"It's nothing like that," Mom said, exchanging a smile with Tina. "In fact, it's not bad news at all."

I fidgeted, annoyed that she'd frightened me. "So, what do you have to tell me that's so important?"

You squeezed my hand. "Let her speak."

When she said it, "Tina is my daughter," I felt dizzy and unmoored.

"Then who am I?"

The three of you laughed, but I needed an answer.

"You're my daughter, too, of course."

Something inside me spun rapidly. How could Tina be her daughter? That would make us sisters. If we had another sister, I'd know. Wouldn't I?

"Before I met your dad, I was married to Gene..." Mom went on.

"Your cousin?"

Again, she chuckled. "He's not my cousin. That's what I'm telling you."

I looked over at Tina, recalling how we used to stare at her childhood photos. "Wait a minute," I said, remembering she wasn't alone in those pictures. "What about Steve?"

"He's my son, your brother."

I knew we had an almost-brother—a baby, born before either of us, who had died at only three days old. But now we also had a live, grown-up brother I'd actually met. Steve even had a son my age.

"But why didn't you tell me?"

"I wanted to protect you. It just would have been too much."

I looked at you and you nodded, as though that made perfect sense. Did it actually make sense to you?

"I'm sure this comes as a shock," Tina put in, and I wondered if what I felt was, in fact, shock. There was a new disorienting slant to the world. But, just below that, I sensed a small place of calm. So much about our family had never made sense, including my resemblance to Tina. Now maybe it did.

I gazed at Tina, realizing how much she looked like Mom. The three of us could play one woman in a movie that spanned a lifetime. "Why'd you finally decide to tell me now?"

You answered for her. "When I first came out west, I looked

up Gene. He thought I already knew, so he said something like, 'While I was married to your mother...'"

"Once Andra heard that," Mom interrupted you to add, "Daddy and I figured there was no hiding it from you."

Now that I knew, I found it easy to remember every slip-up and hint. The times I'd seen Mom pore over Tina's letters, then quickly tuck them in her apron pocket when she caught me watching. The way she referred to Steve as Stevie like a little boy.

I thought back to a trip Mom, Dad, and I took to Disneyland with Steve and his son Blaine. Blaine and I went on the rides together and played hide-and-seek between our adjoining rooms at the hotel, crawling into the headboards that opened like cabinets to store extra pillows.

"How old are you again?" he'd asked on our last day together.

"Nine," I told him. "Why?"

"No reason."

At the time, I assumed Blaine thought I seemed younger because I was small for my age, but now I understood that he asked the question because he knew what I didn't. He was marveling at the strangeness of having an aunt who had no idea that's who she was. An aunt who could fit inside a headboard.

Details like these kept coming, as though I'd been keeping a neat file of unexplainable memories to sort out at some later date. I remembered the summer I was eleven, when Tina and her husband Howie came to stay with us for a night. At some point, I overheard Howie talking on the phone as he bounced his baby, Herman, on his lap.

"A few more days," he said. "We're visiting Tina's mom, then we're heading to Westchester to spend the rest of the week with my folks."

When are they visiting Tina's mom? I'd wondered as I joined

him at the dinette table. I decided he must have meant after they left us.

"I want you to meet my mom," I'd just caught Tina saying, and then quickly explained it away to myself. Apparently, I had always done that. Did that mean, somewhere inside me, I'd actually almost known?

When Mom and Gene divorced, I learned that afternoon, they asked seven-year-old Steve who he'd like to live with. He picked his father and the two of them moved to Las Vegas. Mom raised Tina on her own for a few years before sending her to live with them.

"Wasn't that hard, letting her go?" I asked later, when Mom and I were alone in our room getting ready for bed.

"Of course. Tina was my baby, just like you."

She meant that lovingly, I knew, but the words shook me. For the first time, it felt possible that she could choose to let go of me too. "Then why did you do it?"

"Tina missed her father and brother, so Daddy and I thought she'd be happier in Vegas. She also got rashes and had terrible allergies, which Gene said cleared up right after she arrived."

Maybe that made sense, I thought as I lay under the stiff sheets of my hotel bed. But what didn't was that, while Steve and Tina were still little kids, they became a secret. Three thousand miles away from their mother, they were no longer allowed to call her Mom.

A wave of guilt rose up in me as though I was somehow responsible, even though it had all happened long before I was born. I suppose I was used to feeling that way, afraid as I was in some barely articulated place that it was me, my very existence, that had made everything so hard for you.

Chapter Fourteen

Toward the end of the summer I spent in Berkeley when I was twenty-three, I took the scenic drive up Highway One, with two of my housemates, to visit Tina and her family. By then, she and Howie had a scruffy plot of land near Mendocino and were the parents of six. They lived in two narrow trailers and a spillover living room—a worn couch and a few folding chairs under the open sky.

Soon after we arrived, Howie told us he was taking off with their second oldest, Joey, who was eleven then, to participate in a peace march. I saw my friends' relief, just as I'd seen their alarm at Howie's long uncombed hair and feral beard. But I'd counted on his gentleness to ease the time with Tina. I know she was really kind and generous to you, and I loved her for that. But I found her overwhelming and hard to get to know.

"I wish you were staying," I whispered as Howie hugged me goodbye.

"Someone's got to save the world," he said.

After Howie left, we joined Tina in the outdoor living room and watched her kids chase one another and play. As she often did, Tina free-associated aloud.

"Someday, I'm hoping we'll inherit enough money to put a little house on this land. That would be nice for the kids, and for me too, having a door to close. There's just so many of us." She gazed fondly at the baby in her lap. "I don't even know how I wound up with Davy."

After a while, I suggested to my housemates that they drive through the redwood forest while I spent time with my family.

"You'll be okay?" my friend Anne asked as we stood by her car.

I didn't know how to explain the hope I held out for finding a way to connect with Tina, or what got touched inside me from seeing those open-hearted children who were—through blood, genetics, resemblance—part of me. "I'll be fine."

I found thirteen-year-old Herman getting high inside one of the trailers. He passed me the joint and I took a long toke, wondering only vaguely if I should try setting a better example. Reluctantly, I joined Tina in the yard again where she continued to talk and talk. I drifted in and out, but when she said your name, she had my full attention.

"The week of the murders, Gracie, who was two then, cried inconsolably for an entire day. I had no idea what was upsetting her, but then we learned what happened and I put it together. Children are very psychic, you know?"

My mind leapt to Petey, a parakeet I'd had in ninth grade. I'd let that sweet bird out of his cage, and he'd crawl all over me while I did my homework. One afternoon, I was at a friend's house when I felt a sudden sense of dread. Something bad had happened to Petey. I rushed home and discovered he'd broken his neck trying to climb backwards through his plastic ladder.

Now I wondered what was wrong with me that I could intuit the death of a parakeet, yet have absolutely no inkling that my pregnant sister, my brother-in-law, and little nephew were in danger. If I'd been more present, more attuned to you, maybe you'd all still be alive. I had Dad's credit card for emergencies. Why didn't I recognize the emergency?

"Joey saw her spirit," Tina continued as four-year-old Naomi came over and squeezed between us. "He was in the car with Howie when he saw a woman shimmering on the side of the road by the trees. 'Look, an angel,' he said to Howie. 'An angel lady.' It was just a little while after the murders, so Howie figured it must be Angie."

I ran my fingers through Naomi's fine hair and nodded. Of course your spirit came to Joey rather than me. He was off with his dad, attempting to save the world. Who had I ever saved? Not you. Not the people you loved. Not even my damn parakeet.

When I returned to New York, it felt like you were even farther away. You stopped visiting me in my sleep. In the one dream I had about you in the months that followed, you didn't even appear. I dreamt I was alone in our house in Far Rockaway when I came upon a cloth bag I knew to be yours. From inside, I pulled a cross-stitch sampler with just a small section completed. This was her life, my dream-self thought, moving forward stitch by stitch. Clearly, you had intended to come back to your work. Your needle was there, threaded and waiting, tucked into the cloth.

"Andra never finishes anything she starts," I remember Mom saying. But I was the one who left abandoned projects all over the house. Half-filled notebooks, a needlepoint canvas with just a sliver done, novels facedown and forgotten with only a chapter or two to go. Now, after a quick glimpse of my grief in a San Francisco courtroom, I'd deserted that project too.

Tina and I didn't speak often that year, but one afternoon we lingered on the phone, Davy crying in the background, as she described the health benefits of miso to me. As usual, there were few pauses in her soliloquy, so I did a kind of surfing as she talked, riding some of the waves in her ocean of thoughts while letting others wash over me.

She was in the midst of a complicated ramble I could barely follow when I heard her say, "You know, Angie was molested by a neighbor when she was only ten."

"What? I never heard that."

"Well, she was. When she tried to tell Edie and Lenny, they sent her away."

Tina had that wrong, I thought. I was six when they first sent you away, which meant you were twelve. But then I flashed on an early memory of waking to find Mom across the room in your bed. My birthday was coming up and, for several mornings, she turned to me, her body stretched beneath your quilt, to ask, "How's my four-year-old?" I wanted her to wait, to not call me that until my actual birthday, but the day I finally said so aloud, she laughed. "Today *is* your birthday, Ona-leh."

Now, twenty years later, I wondered why she'd started sleeping in your bed. Where were you? I had a vague sense that I'd been told you were still at summer camp. But, by my birthday in late September, school would've already been underway.

When I tuned back in to Tina, she'd moved on to something else.

"You know Lenny was her dad, right?"

"Huh? Who?"

"Angie. Lenny was her father."

"What are you talking about?" Lenny was my father. Of course he was yours too. Your adopted father.

Tina sighed, impatient with me. "He was her biological father. Your uncle told Angie that your father and her mother went at it one night behind the bar. Lenny was Angie's dad. It's no surprise, really. She looked just like him."

My mind reeled. To me, you had always looked like family, like ours. But I figured that came from intimacy and shared history. Mom even used to say as much. People who live together start to resemble each other after a while.

For the first time, I was struck by the genuine oddness of your adoption story. A woman had entered Dad's bar and somehow it came up in their conversation that she had a six-month-old baby she needed to give up. Were our parents already considering adoption? Possibly. They'd lost three-day-old Peter a few years earlier. Mom had also suffered two miscarriages. Still, none of that changed how strange it was that Dad and your birthmother initiated the exchange in a bar.

Angie was his, I thought, certain of it. It was the affair that had started in the bar. Immediately, I began to doubt myself. If the bar was the giveaway, why wasn't that detail kept secret? It's too ludicrous, I decided. Knowing our frugal father, he saw a way to adopt a child while avoiding expensive agency or lawyer fees.

Finally, I invited myself home to Far Rockaway for a weekend. The facts behind your conception may have been scandalous and hurtful, but they were also thirty years old. Surely, we could talk about it now.

Friday night, I sat with Dad through *Miami Vice* and the news. As we passed a bag of pretzels between us, I kept thinking about what a homebody he was. The longer I sat beside him, the less likely Tina's story seemed.

Still, the next morning, after Mom left for her aerobics class, I joined him at the dinette table where he was rewiring a second-hand lamp.

"Dad? I was wondering...Can I ask you something?"

I watched him work, brow furrowed, hands steady and sure. Did I really need to know if he'd cheated on Mom all those years ago?

"What's on your mind, O.?"

Somehow, I couldn't not ask. "Dad, Tina said something to me recently. Was Angie your daughter? You know, biologically?"

"Ah, this again." Without looking up, he waved me off. "Leave it to Tina to plant that idea in your head."

"But..."

"You remember the time Andra ran away and locked herself in some apartment?" He glanced at me, his hands busy tightening wires.

"Sort of." I had a vague recollection of Dad having to coax you, through a locked door, to come home with him. I wasn't told this story, but had picked it up the way I gathered most information as a child. Through clipped phrases, exchanged looks, words whispered around patches of Yiddish.

"Andra was on this kick then. She kept at me. 'Just say you're my father and I'll come out.' Finally, I said, 'Alright, I'm your father.' I'd raised her, so I wasn't lying."

"So, you're not her birth father?"

"Come on, O. You know she was adopted."

I studied the familiar lines of his face. Worry lines. Of course I knew that. I also knew our practical, dependable father was not the kind of man to get swept up in a fling.

Yet, the following afternoon, out to lunch with Mom, the question slipped from my lips again. I held my breath, braced for the dramatic scene I'd surely unleashed, but her response was calm, musing, as though I'd asked for her take on the plot of a novel.

"That never occurred to me, but I don't think so. Your dad's not that way. And anyway, Andra was such a big girl. She looked nothing like us."

I was on the subway, heading back to Brooklyn, when I realized that what Mom said made no sense. You wouldn't have been built like her if you were Dad's daughter with another woman. You'd have had a body like your birthmother's, or maybe like Grandma Ann's. Dad's mother had been nothing if not zaftig.

Was it true then? Were you and I related by blood? Tina had mentioned an uncle. She had to have meant Manny, but I couldn't turn to him for answers. He died of cancer in November 1982, the same year we lost you.

Back in my Park Slope apartment, I dug out old photos of you next to Dad, next to me. Away from our parents, the idea began to shed its gravity. As a mystery, it was intriguing, even comforting. Having it to ponder gave me one small way to keep you near.

Chapter Fifteen

When your death certificate finally arrived in the mail, I learned there had been a funeral in San Francisco. It was held at Driscoll's Mortuary Chapel on April 19, 1982. Had our parents been aware of it? It didn't seem so. On the document, their names were filled in, but their places of birth, along with your ethnicity, were marked *Unknown*. Ray's mother must have arranged the service. "Informant: Georgianna Boggs, mother-in-law."

"Andrea Susan Gritz." Squeezed above *Andrea*: *Jane Doe #3*. Above *Susan*: *A.K.A. Angie Boggs*. "Cause of Death: Apparent ligature strangulation.... Injury Information: Homicide."

I folded the paper and tucked it back in its envelope. Your death I knew plenty about. What I needed was information on your life.

A few days later, certificate and a notarized letter in hand, I entered the attendance office at Scholar's Academy in Rockaway Park where, in a quick unceremonious transaction, I was handed a bright blue folder with your name on the tab. I felt tempted to sit down right there on the floor and pore through it. Instead, I slipped the folder into my backpack and returned to my friend's car. There, on my lap, my pack became a living thing. I thought of the heavy box that had contained Mom's ashes. I thought of Jeannie perched on a couch inside her magic bottle on the TV show we'd watched as kids.

"This is going on your PERMANENT RECORD," teachers used to yell when someone in the class misbehaved. It was the ultimate threat, yet I remember believing it was a made up thing, meant to scare kids into obedience. But when I got home that afternoon, the papers I pulled from my backpack were copies of your actual permanent record from kindergarten through eighth grade.

The top page was an attendance log, beginning in 1961 when you first entered the public school system. Before that, you attended Carol Play School. A sweet name. The name of a place where they don't let bad things happen.

Soon enough, though, bad things did happen, according to what Tina told me on the phone years before. Molested at ten and sent away. Now, I scanned the log for 1966 and saw you were marked absent nineteen and a half times that year. A full month of school days unaccounted for.

Turning the page, I found a checklist titled *Personality,* with one column for kindergarten, your last year as our parents' only child, and one for first grade, the year you became my big sister.

In both grades, you received S's for satisfactory in all your subjects. You *played well with others, generally worked with confidence,* were *relatively free of nervous habits.* You also *required direction* and *occasionally evaded responsibility.* The differences were: in kindergarten, you were *satisfied with a reasonable amount of attention.* But, in first grade, you required *an inordinate amount of attention.* In kindergarten, you were *moderately aggressive.* But, the following year, you were *over aggressive, fighting frequently.*

I consciously slowed my breath. These kinds of shifts were to be expected with a new baby at home. It was natural for there to have been a period of adjustment for an older sibling. But while I knew this was true generally, I also knew that, in our home, nothing got better with time.

Moving to the next packet, I learned that, after those first two years, you earned mostly F's for fair in your subjects. It stayed that way through junior high.

Finally, under *Guidance Data*, I came upon something other than check boxes and fill-in-the-blanks. Brief handwritten statements for fifth and then sixth grade.

"Limited span of attention. Child is adopted, seems to bother her."

"Andra is adopted, and it bothers her—feels mother loves 'real' sister, not her."

Real sister. As I read those words my body warmed like in a blush, though instead of rising to the surface of my skin, the heat radiated from deep within me. Can a person blush in her bowels?

When we were young, birthmothers were referred to as real mothers. "Do you ever want to meet your real mother?" I remembered asking as we lay across from each other one night. "Nah, what for?"

But *"real" sister*? The phrasing was so odd the teacher had put the word in quotes. Did you believe I was not only more loved, but more real? Did I?

Shame is an eraser, I wrote earlier in these pages to you, meaning that, in my shame, I'd let my memories fade. But there was more to it than that. Since my youngest years, I'd held onto the sense I'd had of you as simply on pause if you weren't in my presence, like a television character between episodes. That erasure had allowed me to cope in a home where my unearned privilege made me feel both culpable and safe. It proved useful again when I lost you in such an unimaginable way.

But you were real, of course. Beyond my patchy fading memory and plastic bin of photos. A person who had lived, and suffered, out in the actual world.

"Very helpful, considerate child," the paragraph by the

guidance counselor continued. "Needs constant love, encouragement, and praise."

What child doesn't? I thought angrily. What parent, adoptive or otherwise, doesn't owe every one of their children exactly that?

Exhausted, I felt an urge to gather those papers back into their cheery folder, stuff them in a drawer, and lie down for a nap. Instead, I reached for another packet.

A page titled *Notes* spanned from kindergarten through to eighth grade. On each line, your teachers had filled in clipped, unsettling comments.

November 4, 1963, second grade: "Listless--bizarre behavior."

November 10, 1964: "Frequent absences, colds, upset stomach. Listless child, odd behavior."

Bizarre, odd. No further explanation, no examples. Just those words.

A single entry for 1966 stated "No recurrence of last year's problem," though the one note for 1965 said you'd poked yourself in the eye with a pencil and a compress had been applied.

February 21, 1967, "Bright but not working up to capacity—seems unhappy at times."

March 12, 1969, "Student has seizures, on medication."

March 28, 1969, "Discharged to hospital." Underneath, penciled lightly in parenthesis so that I nearly missed it, "Creedmoor."

I stopped breathing.

March 28, 1969. Was that the day I'd walked home from first grade and found you gone? "There are special schools for girls who keep looking for trouble."

But Creedmoor was no school. It was a state-run mental institution, infamous over the years for cruel treatments, medically induced comas, and the frequent escape of criminally insane inmates. For children growing up in Queens as we did, it was where the bogeyman lived.

I thought of all the days you had missed in fifth grade. Were you in Creedmoor then too? I glanced back at the notation for 1966. "No recurrence of last year's problem." No answer there.

The final note on the page was dated October 10, 1969. "Child marked present in school, but not attending class here." Your whereabouts were again faintly penciled in and in parenthesis. "Youth House." I had no idea what that was.

Typing the words into a search box, I felt a stone of dread harden in my stomach at what I might uncover. At the same time, it was a relief to have a task. Piecing together clues online gave me whole minutes to look away from this new picture of you as a twelve-year-old child, the heavy gates of Creedmoor clanking shut at your back. Whole minutes when I wasn't working to metabolize the unbearable thought that our parents had put you there.

You were at boarding school. That's all I was ever told. You were gone. That's all I let myself feel. Understandable when all this first began and I was just a little girl. But how did I get stuck there, with a little girl's grasp of what had happened, until now?

In my fourteenth summer, when Mom finally told me about her other children, I was relentless with my questions. How come they sent Tina away? Why did they keep Steve and her a secret? Didn't they care about how that made our half-siblings feel? The answers I got were rarely satisfying, but I kept probing. Why then had I never asked those kinds of questions on your behalf? I didn't ask our parents. I didn't ask you. I waited until no one alive could answer my questions before I allowed myself anywhere near the jagged and dangerous truth.

Over the coming weeks and months, I buried my desk beneath printouts of digitized articles, and piled my nightstand with battered library discards and yellowed paperbacks. Do you remember the nickname you and Ray gave me the one time you visited me at SUNY Purchase? It started when I'd pointed out the library on campus and mentioned spending way too much time there. "Well, excuse me, Miss Educated," you'd said. Listening back through the years, I can hear pride beneath your teasing. But in the moment, it had felt like an accusation. Who was I to move so far past the sister I once worshiped? Now, here I was, your bookish little sister, attempting to educate my way back to you.

I contacted Creedmoor Psychiatric Center and learned you were there from April 24 to June 6, 1969. *A voluntary admission*, the letter called it. Later, I'd read in a book by Nina Bernstein, whose articles I'd found on the reform school in Hudson, that all children under fourteen placed in state mental hospitals were designated as such, with no rights "... separate from those of the adults who had placed them there."

April 24, 1969. Your school record had it as March 28 and, for a while, this discrepancy confused me. But then, waking with a start one morning, I saw how it could fit. There was the day Mom claimed you wouldn't be there when I got home from school, which turned out to be a warning—had Dad driven you to the gates and been unable to go through with it? And then there was the day, some weeks later, when I walked in the door to find you really gone.

Springtime. You should have been playing double Dutch, browsing in record shops, eating pizza at Gino's with friends. The previous spring, our friend and upstairs neighbor Lisa had been killed. "We had a little accident," Mom told me as she stood at the sink squeezing out a sponge. Dad, as far as I recalled, said nothing. You were the only one in our house who cried that night. The only one to have a sane response.

"Often an entire family is crazy," Susanna Kaysen writes in

Girl, Interrupted, her memoir about the years she spent in a psychiatric facility as a teenager in the late sixties. "But since an entire family can't go into the hospital, one person is designated as crazy and goes inside."

With no other clue than the words *Youth House*, it took me a while to uncover where exactly you had been sent next. Finally, I found a mention of the place in a piece about Lee Harvey Oswald. At the age of thirteen, Kennedy's future assassin had been sent to Youth House in the Bronx for chronic truancy.

As I dug further, I willed the phone to ring, the doorbell to sound, anything to pull me away from this heartbreaking work. But you had whispered *180* to me. I truly believed this. Wherever that took me, you wanted me to go.

Youth House, renamed Spofford Juvenile Center two years before your arrival, turned out to be New York City's main maximum-security juvenile detention center. I couldn't imagine what crime you could have possibly committed that would land you in such a place. Were there arrest records I could track down?

Instinctively, I reached out to my old teenage crush, Danny, who had lived at the Gustav Hartman Home for Children when I knew him. He put me in touch with another schoolmate of ours who'd also lived in the group home. Marnie had been briefly held at Spofford before her arrival in our hometown. She was eight years old.

"Correction officers fingerprinted you when you arrived at Spofford," she told me on the phone. "They strip searched you..."

"You were strip searched? At eight?"

"It was jail," she reminded me. "They strip-searched everybody. It was *jail* jail."

Because Marnie was essentially parentless, the court considered her a PINS, a Person In Need of Supervision. Orphans, runaways, truants, and kids deemed "incorrigible" were all labeled PINS. This was New York's euphemism for charging you with a status offense, a crime that wouldn't be considered a crime if committed by an adult. Due to the Wayward Minor Act, a state law on the books since 1923, status offenses were punishable by imprisonment. I didn't need to track down court records to find out why you'd been locked up. A parent, when reporting a child missing, could request a warrant for that child's arrest.

Again and again, I read of instances where parents jettisoned their children. In a June 1968 *Good Housekeeping* article on the "highly publicized runaway explosion," sixteen-year-old Susan returned home after a single night on the street only to be asked by her mother, "What are you doing in my house?" In Nina Bernstein's *The Lost Children of Wilder*, twelve-year-old Shirley's father brought her to court to request that she be "put away." In a 1973 *New York Times* article, "Failures in the System of Detention," thirteen-year-old Jessica was asked by a counselor why she was back at Spofford after her case had been dismissed. She replied, "My mother wouldn't take me home."

This, I imagined, was how it had happened at our house. While I was at school filling out a worksheet on vocabulary words, or outside where my biggest problem was being unable to skate like my friends, Mom answered a ringing phone.

"Ma'am, we have a child in custody who claims she's your daughter."

I could practically hear her sigh, see her lips whiten before she responded in a tight voice. "Well, keep her in custody. We certainly can't handle her here."

Had our parents seen the high walls of Spofford, topped with searchlights and razor wire? Were they told your room would be a locked cell? That the showers and bathroom stalls had no doors?

While Mom read *Harry and the Lady Next Door* with me for the umpteenth time, or Dad pulled my foot to his nose to tease me for having *felly smeet*, did they worry about how you'd stay safe in a place known, above all, for its violence? Or, with no thought at all to what you might be going through, were they simply glad you were gone? I recalled the coldness in Mom's voice and that slap-slap dusting off of her hands when, barely a decade later, she told me you had been killed.

Feels mother loves "real" sister, not her.

Angie, shall I give you the last word in this chapter? "No shit, Sherlock," you used to say.

Chapter Sixteen

The morning after Mom finally told me the truth about her first family, I thought of how I sometimes had flashes of panic, imagining I'd been abandoned. It happened in places like Korvettes when she and Dad sent me to the record department so I wouldn't have to tag along after them as they shopped. For a while, I liked the independence. But at some point, as I flipped through the albums, I'd think, They're not coming. They're done with me. I pictured the store preparing to close around me, the lights going off, the security guard offering to drive me to the police station if I'd wait out his shift. But even as I envisioned the scene and placed myself in it, I never truly believed it would happen. It was a bit like riding a roller coaster or watching a horror movie. The things we do to scare ourselves, fully aware that we're safe.

Now, though, I knew our parents had actually abandoned children. As we went on with our visit like the world hadn't just shifted on its axis, I watched Mom chat with you, Howie, and Tina at meals, and pull four-year-old Herman and two-year-old Joey into her arms. They're her grandchildren, I'd remind myself, and wait to see if I somehow felt differently about her. But she was just Mom, embarrassing me by fussing over whether I'd dressed warmly enough, insisting on buying me a bracelet she saw me admiring in a shop window. She was still the person who knew my deepest secrets. Maybe not my crushes or the small ways I acted out with friends. Those were the things I shared with you. But Mom knew how testy and temperamental I could be, and that, at almost fifteen,

I still cried like a baby—sometimes over hurt feelings, sometimes for no reason, often just to get my way. She was the person I'd wake in the middle of the night when I needed reassuring. The one I was the most myself with, which made it all the more stunning that she'd kept such an enormous secret from me.

Meanwhile, throughout that week, our suddenly large and raucous clan kept breaking off into groups of different combinations. Howie and I strolling with Herman and Joey down Market Street. Mom and I watching the boys in our room while Tina and Howie took you out for birthday drinks.

Earlier that day, I'd given you the card with my poem. "Open it up and see what I wrote," I prompted.

"You wrote this?" you asked with a quick glance at the calligraphy. "When did you learn to do that?"

"Well, no, my friend did the lettering. I wrote the poem. Read it. It's for you."

You opened the card again, but just long enough for Tina to see Kerry's handiwork. "Ona had a friend do that. Isn't it nice?" you said, before dropping it, unread, on the dresser.

On another afternoon, we three sisters had the hotel room to ourselves. The conversation, mostly between you and Tina, quickly turned to sex.

"With Howie it has to be all spiritual. He lights candles and talks about our union being symbolic of all beings' oneness through God."

"It's nothing like that with Big Bear. He's such a huge guy, all we worry about is finding positions where I don't get squashed." You grinned and your eyes fell on me, cross-legged beside you on the bed. "Look at Ona. You don't know what to make of any of this, do you, baby?"

"I understand what you're talking about," I said.

"That's right." You poked at my side. "You're not the angel we thought you were, are you?" This wasn't about sex, but a different kind of secret I'd shared with you. "Ona tried pot with some friends from school," you told Tina, filling her in.

Clearly, you loved knowing I'd stepped out of my goody-two-shoes role for once. You mentioned it often, slyly, in ways Mom wouldn't be able to decode. "My baby sister's growing up. It's like her childhood just went up, poof, in smoke." But Tina had no interest in my adolescent experiments. She watched you carefully as you stood and lifted your blouse to study your tattooed stomach in the mirror: *Property of Big Bear* in dark cursive letters. I glanced at my card on the dresser, which someone had used as a coaster, and realized there was no place in your wild life for a gift as innocent as a birthday poem. I might as well have given you a crayon drawing.

"I'll tell you something I'm proud of," you said to your reflection. "Whenever I've had to do it for money, it was on my own terms. I never used a pimp. Not once."

What can I say about how I felt hearing that? Earlier that year, my crush Danny had asked if I'd like him to kiss me. I felt so unprepared, I answered, "I want you to kiss my guitar," and held the curved body between us, blocking his face from mine. Around this same time, a man had phoned the house looking for you, referring to you as Andra, which meant it had been years since you'd been in touch. I told him I didn't know where you were and, after making small talk for a minute, he said, "So, your sister and I used to sleep together." Before I could figure out how to respond, he asked, "Do you think maybe I could sleep with you sometime?" I'd slammed down the phone, shocked. Now, as you let slip matter-of-factly that you slept with strangers for money, it surprised me for a moment and then simply made sense. I guess what I'm saying is, in most ways, I was a really young fourteen-year-old. At the same time, having you as my sister made me feel jaded too.

Meanwhile, regret, like a faint second heartbeat, pulsed below all of this. I couldn't even think the word *prostitute* without remembering the first time I'd spoken it, when I was only nine and didn't really understand what it meant. What I did know was that Mom loved gossip. I'd seen how it drew her and her girlfriends together, so I decided to try it out. "Andra kind of dresses like a prostitute, right?" I whispered to Mom as a secret between us. But days later, I heard her yell into the phone, "Even your little sister thinks you dress like a two-bit whore!"

You never mentioned it, but somehow word traveled all the way to Uncle Manny in Brooklyn. "You didn't say something mean to hurt your sister, did you?" he asked the next time he came over. As he studied my face, I wanted a rewind button like on a tape recorder. I wanted to go back to the moment I'd said what I did and hit erase.

Now, I watched you reapply your lipstick in the hotel mirror. "You guys hungry at all?" I asked, ready to leave that little room.

Though I'd grown fond of the idea that Steve and Tina were our siblings, and I absolutely loved being an aunt, I was thrilled that you decided to spend our last night with just Mom and me in our room. My original family.

I remember that you washed Mom's hair in the sink. "Ooh, Andra, you're really good at this," she crooned as you massaged the lather into her scalp. I laughed, happy you were getting along.

Afterwards, you joined me on my bed. It felt so familiar to sit gazing at TV, pressed up against you. I recalled one particular time we watched a lineup of sitcoms with our parents when we were younger. You had already started hanging out with guys and smoking cigarettes, and I could feel you drifting away from me. But on that night, you wore a pair of faded, too-short pajamas, revealing the marbly skin of your legs and the mole, like dropped chocolate, on your ankle. Noticing those details made me feel better. Only we get to see her like this, I'd assured myself. She's still mostly ours.

Now, you put an arm around me, I nudged my face into your smoky hair, and we drifted off. That must have been the last time the two of us ever slept curled together like that. The next morning, Mom and I woke to find you gone. Your pants a crumpled ball beneath the bed. My favorite broken-in Levi's, which you had asked for and I hadn't wanted to give up, missing along with you.

"Is she really not even going to say goodbye?" I asked as Mom began to pack furiously. I remembered how glad I'd felt to have a night to ourselves, just the family I was used to. This is us alright, I thought. Typical us.

When I started to cry, Mom sighed. "Oh, Ona," she said. "Don't waste your tears."

Chapter Seventeen

The final page in the packet of school records I'd acquired at Scholar's Academy was an undated letter from the State Department of Social Welfare in Hudson, New York.

"We understand that the above-named girl, who was recently committed to our care, attended your school. May we have the following information as soon as possible..."

By the time I held that letter in my hands, I'd read Nina Bernstein's articles and knew that, though the New York State Training School for Girls looked from the outside like a pleasant country boarding school, it was, in many ways, as brutal as Spofford. A place where washing floors and working in the laundry took priority over class time. Where the most common punishment for even minor infractions was solitary confinement in a padded windowless cell.

When I read all this on that late afternoon after I'd called the town library in Hudson and set this long overdue quest in motion, I didn't doubt that any of it was true. At the same time, I couldn't help feeling there must be more to the story. In our bin of old family photos, there are plenty of pictures of you as an unhappy teenager, narrowing your eyes and looking sullenly off in the distance, clenching your jaw in an obvious attempt not to cry. But Angie, those were all taken at home. In the photos from our visits to Hudson, you seem confident and serene. You look like a girl who finally knows she's loved.

For a while, I thought that meant things must have been even worse for you in our house than I'd realized. That it was a relief to be anywhere—even an archaic reform school—other than home. Then, after I learned about Creedmoor and Spofford, I figured Hudson must have been the least of the evils, the photos documenting your relief at having moved on from those other two versions of hell.

As I write this, I imagine you're giving me your sly, crooked smile. I've earned it. I've solved the puzzle and uncovered the one bright spot behind the stone walls of that prison for twelve to sixteen-year-old girls.

When I first came upon descriptions of what inmates called the Racket, in Nina Bernstein's *The Lost Children of Wilder*, it seemed like just one more source of violence. She tells of a sexual assault in a bathroom, of a girl getting cut for refusing to join. It was from a different book, one listed in her bibliography, that I learned there was another side to the Racket and recognized it as the gift it must have been.

Does the name Rose Giallombardo sound familiar? Did you meet her? Giallombardo wrote *The Social World of Imprisoned Girls* after gathering data and interviewing inmates at the New York State Training School and two similar institutions in other parts of the country. She did this work between April 1968 and April 1973. Whole chapters are filled with quotes from the teenage inmates of Hudson, all anonymous. Of course I couldn't help but listen for your voice as I pored through that book. I drew an asterisk next to "Don't knock it if you've never tried it." A circle around "It was all thrown up in my face!"

One girl described campus names. "It's a name that fits the person. You might be Dimples because you have dimples. You might be called Shyness because you're shy..."

I read through the list and ruled out Double Eyes since you

never wore glasses, and China, guessing the name belonged to an Asian American girl. Maybe you were Heatwave, Sunny, or Tenderness. On some level, I knew it was pointless to search for you in this way. I didn't even know if Giallombardo's months at the Training School actually overlapped with yours. Nonetheless, I kept at it, looking for hints of your presence in the population tables, taking notes on what I found.

"Of the 205 inmates, two = Jewish, & one is listed as having no religion."

You could have been one of the two Jewish girls Giallombardo met, I believed. But months later, I received a scan of your listing in the commitment ledger from the State Archives and discovered that, while our parents felt it was important enough to have the word *adoptive* squeezed into the small spaces above their names, the boxes for religious faith were left blank. I could go on for a while about that choice, having learned through my research of alternative out-of-home placements in privately run Jewish centers. One was the Pleasantville Cottage School where, my old crush Danny reminded me on the phone, he had lived before coming to the group home in Far Rockaway. Another, Hawthorne-Cedar Knolls, is documented as having had a quota for Jewish children of 60%. Of the 28,000 children in need of placement in the state, only 4% were Jewish. I know. Enough stats and quotas, Miss Educated. Get to the promised good stuff. But let me just finish with this: these sought-after centers had twice as many openings as they had Jewish kids to fill them. You would have been guaranteed a spot somewhere that offered classes and counseling services in a well-kept, safe environment, if only our parents had asked.

As it was, you were in the state reformatory in Hudson where one housemother maintained order in her cottage with a baseball bat, and a dentist named R. Mary Wend—the very one, I'm sure, who pulled your front tooth—filled inmates' mouths with improvised braces made of bamboo.

The one saving grace? The secret and forbidden world of the Racket with its gender role-play. Its romantic relationships. The protective and devoted families you all formed to take care of each other and yourselves.

"Most everybody here belongs to a family," a Hudson inmate explained to Giallombardo. "It makes you feel like you're a part of things. Plus you trust people more—the ones that are in your family. They're there when you need them."

I know that the kids in the Racket who took the role of butches swaggered through campus in boy's sneakers with extra socks to make their ankles look thicker. That, since pants weren't allowed, they kept the zippers of their skirts partly open so they could tuck their hands in those makeshift pockets. But you, my love, were a femme. In my favorite photo of the two of us in Hudson, you're wearing a flattering sundress with a pattern of pink circles. For the first time ever, you have on makeup. Your highlighted hair is styled in a flip.

"Hey, this is my brother," you might have said to another inmate at some point. But the sibling you introduced wouldn't have been a kid like me, strolling the deceptively manicured grounds on visiting day with no understanding of where exactly I'd come. It would have been a teenage girl made into a brother through longing and imagination and the time-honored rituals of the Racket. Rituals as real to you as the high walls and heavy doors that kept you in that place.

I know about "True Butches and Femmes," girls who identified as lesbians out in the wider world, and "Trust-to-Be's," girls who were, as we'd say today, gay for the stay. I know that H.O.L.L.A.N.D on a love letter, or an *issue* as you called it, meant *Hope Our Love*

Lasts And Never Dies, S.W.M.T.K. meant *Sealed With My Tongue Kiss*, and T.H.A.W. meant *True Husband And Wife*.

Uncovering this part of your world away from me allowed me to feel like I was talking to you again. I also felt tremendous relief to have found this one thing, in the mostly dark chasm between the two of us touching tongues as children and you meeting Ray, that consisted of love.

According to Rose Giallombardo, over 84% of the girls she interviewed in Hudson participated in the Racket, but I didn't need that statistic to convince me that you were someone's wife, lover, sister, or mother in your time there. You taught me the magic of make-believe as soon as I was old enough to be your playmate. It was your first means of escape and then it became mine.

And you know what else, Angie? You once actually gave me a hint.

This must have been shortly after you'd returned from Hudson. You lay on your bed, flipping through a magazine, while I made up a game in my head where I sang lead in an all-girl group.

"Andra?" I asked. "If you had your own rock band, what would you call it?"

I could tell by how quickly you answered that you had thought about this too.

"The Racketeers," you said.

Chapter Eighteen

One night, soon after I'd started eleventh grade, I picked up the phone by my bed to call a friend and heard you crying on the line.

"He hit me with his car, Daddy."

"Angie? Are you okay?" I asked.

"Get off the phone, Ona," Dad said sternly.

Shaking, I dropped the receiver in its cradle like it was giving off shocks. I couldn't believe you'd been hit by a car. Like Lisa. But you must be okay, I told myself. You were talking. I felt sure that, any minute now, Dad would call out that you were ready to speak to me. "I'm fine, baby, just a little banged up," you'd say.

But ten minutes passed, then twenty. I put the phone to my ear and heard a dial tone. I thought maybe Dad was taking some time to absorb the news. Finally, I went out to the TV area where I found him watching *Barney Miller*. Mom, as far as I knew, was up in the Catskills with a friend.

"Dad, how's Angie? What happened to her?"

He sighed and shook his head. "She got hit pretty bad, poor kid, but she'll be okay. Your mother is with her now."

For a moment, I wondered how Mom had made it to San Francisco so quickly from Upstate New York. Then I got it. This didn't just happen, and Mom hadn't been on a trip to the Catskills at all. She'd gone straight to California days ago. All that time, Mom and Dad both knew about your accident and chose not to tell me.

"Great, just great," I yelled and stormed to my room.

I put an Elton John album on the turntable and threw the needle down. "Your Sister Can't Twist (But She Can Rock 'n Roll)" came on, and I realized I had no idea what you could and couldn't do now. The beat of the next song, "Saturday Night's Alright for Fighting," matched my own thrumming fury perfectly. I turned the volume up as high as it could go.

Finally, my door blew open. "Ona! Why is that blasting?"

"Why? I can't believe you're asking me that!"

"This is just selfishness, O."

I turned the music off completely, but screamed as though I still had to be heard above the blare. "I'm sick and tired of secrets."

For just a moment, as I watched him retreat from the room, his arthritic back hunched, I understood that he'd chosen the right word for me. *Selfish.* You were lying in pain in a far-off hospital bed, yet I'd managed to make this about me. Not that I lingered there. In the coming days, I learned the details of the accident. How you'd been walking home at night when a policeman called to you. How you'd stepped into the street to talk to him through his open window and were hit by another car. But I was so practiced at not thinking about the precarious life you lived all those miles away from us, it seemed almost like a fictional story.

Dad and I weren't used to spending time alone together, but by the end of that week, we'd gotten the hang of talking to each other. One night, while the two of us ate dinner at McDonald's, I confided in him that something I'd always envied about you was the spark that made everyone love you.

He studied my face. "You've got it wrong, O. That's you. She's always envied that about you."

I smiled, flattered that he thought so, but I knew he was wrong. People out in the world, guys especially, were drawn to you. Sure, Mom and Dad loved me, but that didn't mean there was anything special about me. Parent-to-child love was automatic.

When we got home, our conversation was still on my mind. Parent-to-child love should be a given, but I had so few memories of Mom acting loving toward you. When you got your first period and she huddled with you in the bathroom. When she pulled out the ironing board on a school morning because you'd asked her to iron your hair. But these moments and gestures were exceptions, and I knew they shouldn't be. Nor should either of us be as surprised as we were that Mom had flown out to be with you now.

"I was so touched when I woke up and saw Ma sitting in the chair next to my bed," you said every time we spoke. "She'd been there all night. I couldn't believe it."

I wanted to say, "Of course she came. Why wouldn't she?" But I knew I'd just be pretending we were a different kind of family.

That November, Steve got married. Mom, Dad, and I went to Las Vegas for the wedding. We spent a few days with Steve and his new wife Terri, and it turned out their taste in music and books matched mine. The three of us could talk for hours.

One evening, I sat on the counter, chatting with Terri while she made dinner. "Don't tell your brother," she said, reaching behind the toaster for a pack of cigarettes.

"I won't," I promised, feeling the familiarity of the moment deep in my bones.

From there, we flew to San Francisco. "She's here!" I sang out, spotting you as soon as we entered the hotel lobby. But my throat tightened when you limped over, leaning heavily on a crutch.

"I'm almost done with this third leg, but the doctor thinks I'll probably always limp."

"Well," I said, trying to sound upbeat. "Now we'll look even more like sisters."

We dropped our stuff in our room and took a walk down Geary Street. At some point, a guy, waiting at the light in a beat-up convertible, shouted, "Check out the tits on the girl with the crutch!"

I laughed and, for a moment, actually felt reassured by this goofy proof that a woman with a limp, and even a crutch, could be considered sexy. I'd also managed to convince myself that things were better between you and Mom after your hospital stay, but the guy's comment pulled the stopper off her fury.

"You see?" she said. "Everywhere you go, it's the same."

"How is this my fault?" you asked.

"Well, look at you. Look how you dress."

From what I remember, you were in jeans and a tight-fitting t-shirt. I might have been wearing the same thing, and Mom wouldn't have said a word.

When we got back to the hotel, Dad holed up in the lobby while the rest of us changed for dinner. Hovering ghostlike over the next half hour was what it could have been. A mother and her two girls chatting and confiding as we dressed and primped for a night out.

As it was, Mom rummaged in her suitcase for something for you to wear, doing it with an air of having to clean up a spill.

Watching her from the bed, you cupped a breast in each hand. "You think I chose these, Ma? The truth is, they're kind of embarrassing."

It pained me to see you sitting there in your bra, willing your body to shrink to a size that would meet with her approval. "She can't help that Marilyn Monroe was her birthmother," I joked, as though that could smooth things over.

Finally, you decided to change the subject altogether. "You want to see something beautiful?"

I joined you on the bed, and you placed two rings in my palm:

slim, gold, with lines of inlaid pearl and a tiny hook and eye to connect them. A wedding set so delicate and perfect it seemed we should whisper in its presence.

"I got these from a guy who wants to marry me."

This wasn't Ray, of course. Not yet. "Do you want to marry him?"

"I'm not sure, baby. I'm thinking about it."

Suddenly, Mom snatched the rings from my hand and closed her fist around them. "I'll hold onto these," she said brusquely.

"Ma!" you protested. "Those are mine."

"You'll just lose them or give them away," Mom said, snapping them into her change purse. "I'm holding them for safekeeping."

"Did you see that?" you asked me, near tears. "She stole my rings!"

There it was. A simple plea in your flashing brown eyes. *Take my side here. Have my back.* It was just a moment, but I see it now as a portal I could have walked through. You were in the right and we both knew it. Maybe, as Mom said, you would have lost the rings, but they were yours to do with what you wanted.

Yet the sixteen-year-old girl I was then barely wavered. "She's just holding them for you," I said with a shrug. I saw myself as keeping the peace, as though there was any peace to preserve in the charged air of that hotel room. I believed I hadn't taken sides, even as I aligned myself with Mom.

Once, years before, you'd said to me on the phone, "I'm sorry I haven't been a better sister."

It wasn't connected to anything we had been talking about. You just put it in there by itself, like something you'd been meaning to say.

"That's okay," I'd responded. "You're a good sister."

But, even as I gave that meager answer, I knew I had at least as much to apologize for. I may have kept your secrets when we were small, but there were no stakes there. No one was the wiser. In the nineteen precious years I got to be your sister, I never once risked my safe place in our family by standing up for you.

Chapter Nineteen

The year after my summer in Berkeley, I turned twenty-five. Your age—a detail I noted but didn't linger on. I was teaching English composition as an adjunct at NYU. My poems had begun appearing in literary journals. And I discovered that, while I would never be the beauty you had been, there were moments when I'd feel lovely and even powerful. My uneven legs hidden beneath a soft flowing skirt, a microphone amplifying my voice as I recited stanzas I'd said aloud so many times in the making of them I knew them by heart.

I had a new boyfriend then, Richard, with dark wavy hair, expressive eyes, and a compact athletic build. A few months into our relationship, his father died of a heart attack. At the funeral, while Richard stood at the podium reading a tribute he had written the night before, I broke into sobs. I barely knew my boyfriend's father, but tears and snot streamed down my face, and I wailed loud enough that people squirmed around in their seats to stare. It's because Richard's hurting, I told myself.

The next day, I rode to the train station in the backseat of Richard's mother's car. Beside her, he fidgeted, flicking the lid on the ashtray in his armrest, playing with the buttons on the radio. He caught Mick Jagger singing "Angie," and I burst into tears again.

"I'm fine," I insisted between sobs when, frowning, Richard turned toward me, when his mother's worried eyes searched my face in the rearview.

For six years, I had been waiting to feel something about your death. I'd flown across the country in an attempt to find my pain. Now, at last, here it was. A sorrow so close to the surface, all it took was the funeral of an acquaintance, and the refrain of a song I'd heard countless times, for it to come pouring out. But in those moments, my crying was all wrong. It made me seem foolish and self-serving, as though I merely wanted to steal attention away from the freshness and shock of another family's loss.

Embarrassed, I pushed all that grief and longing back down again. It certainly didn't belong in that heartbroken woman's car. As I embarked on my new life with her son, I did so with a growing and unspoken belief that it didn't belong anywhere, except maybe, now and then, on the page.

On my twenty-sixth birthday, I was conscious of the fact that I'd come to an age you never reached. Seven years had passed since you had been killed, which meant that every cell in my body had been replaced since we were last together. I thought this was an interesting concept for a poem, but I never wrote it. Instead, I started a manuscript for a young adult novel I worked on, intermittently, over so many years I eventually had to revise it to include cell phones and Internet. *AWOL* tells the story of fifteen-year-old Sandra who had been adopted at six months from a customer at her father's coffee shop. After a fight with her mother, with whom she's never gotten along, she rides the subway to the famed coffee shop to see a piece of her own history. There, she encounters a community of teen runaways who live with, and are loosely mothered by, a caring but troubled waitress. Sandra stays with her too, and eventually learns that this woman is her birthmother, and that her adopted father and birth father are one and the same.

Not long after I started work on *AWOL*, Richard proposed, apologizing that he couldn't afford to buy me a ring.

"That's okay," I told him. "I've got one."

One phone call to Mom made this true. Through most of our ten-month engagement, I wore half of the delicate bridal set Mom had confiscated from you. While I loved that slender ring, I'd sometimes glance at the small stone glittering on my finger and recall how I'd replaced a portrait of you in an antique picture frame with one of me. I was eleven then, and you were missing as usual. One afternoon—bored, testing—I asked Mom if we could buy a frame for an 8x10 portrait I'd recently posed for in a department store.

"You know, like this," I went on, holding the framed black-and-white photograph of you as a three-year-old that had lived on our parents' bureau since before I was born.

"Just put it in that," she said, giving me the response I'd counted on with both hope and dread. The princess of the family ensuring that her crown still fit, all the while hating herself for the privilege laid atop her head.

I had the wedding ring that completed your set, but when Richard and I shopped for his simple silver band, I decided I wanted one free of history too.

Richard held me tightly against him as we slept and woke me in the morning by singing "Rise and Shine" dearly off key. When I made a lentil soup so thick with barley all the water was absorbed, he taped a note to the pot that said, "Soup, a dollar a slice." But Richard was also difficult to live with. He pouted unless we spent our free afternoons shopping for the things he wanted and our evenings watching the TV shows he liked. He raged and punched holes in our walls, criticized my clothes, my body, my taste in music, the way I spoke to my friends and his. At times, the relationship seemed like a penance, and somehow that felt right to me. As if, by living with a man who was more spoiled and demanding than I was, I could level out the imbalances of the past.

I went back to school for my master's in library science and worked for the New York Public Library until Richard and I had our son. Ethan was a healthy baby with blond hair and an impish smile like yours. Even so, in my disorienting first year as his mom, you, a new mother who had been brutally murdered along with your boy, were far from my mind.

I will say this, though, Angie. I was really struggling then. Somehow, before Ethan's birth, even late in my pregnancy when an extra forty pounds added a waddle to my already awkward walk, I didn't consider how physically demanding, how beyond my capabilities, taking care of an infant would be. When I first tried to nurse, Ethan couldn't reach my breast because of the sloppy cradle my uneven arms made for him. I was finally able to do it by using a tire-shaped nursing pillow that Velcroed to my waist, but I couldn't bathe him without help, or swaddle him, or eat anything more challenging than a breadstick while nursing. Still, I nursed constantly since it turned out to be the only activity that kept him from screaming like he was being dismembered. Hour after hour, I sat in our glider rocker and, for all I was able to do for myself with a baby in my arms, I may as well have been in traction.

Mom came twice a week to spell me and give Ethan his bath, taking two trains and a bus to get to my apartment in Hoboken from where she and Dad now lived on Long Island.

Once, when I marveled at her easy way with the baby, she responded, "Well, I've had a lot of experience. I've raised four children."

I didn't call her on it. Didn't point out that, if the definition of raising children was to see them through to adulthood, she'd only raised one.

"Makes sense," I muttered, telling myself it wasn't worth quibbling over a word choice, and went to take a nap.

During another of Mom's visits, on an unseasonably warm day in November, we ran errands. Ethan, six weeks old then, lay against my chest in his little carrier as I swung the bag containing my purchases.

"Memoirs are very popular," Mom said. She and I often discussed what we were reading, but she'd said this apropos of nothing, adding, "You should write a memoir."

My unfinished manuscript of *AWOL* lay tucked away in a desk drawer, but I had completed a lyrical children's book, which, to my amazement, had been accepted by a major publisher.

"What could I possibly write a memoir about?"

Mom's own favorite books were biographies and autobiographies. She was always happy to share details about the lives of artists, writers, royalty, and rock stars. Meanwhile, my world, in those first weeks of motherhood, felt tiny. Our stroll to the drugstore my big outing for the week.

"I think you've led an interesting life," she answered. "You've been through a lot, you know, with Andra as your sister..."

I froze at this rare mention of you.

"I'm a poet," I said crisply, sounding, I'm sure, as though I saw poetry as the higher art form. But what I really felt was that I could only write about my childhood the way I'd trained myself to consider it. In quick glimpses before I had to turn away.

Chapter Twenty

One weekend, during that year I'd finally begun exploring the details of your life, I attempted to organize my messy hall closet. On the top shelf, I caught sight of a metal case I'd brought home eight years earlier, when I'd cleaned out our parents' Long Island apartment after they died. Inside were slides, but since we didn't own a projector, I'd never seen them. I'd all but forgotten they were there.

Now, I tried to view one by holding it up against the bulb of a lamp, but I could barely make out the shadowy forms. Finally, it dawned on me that all I needed was a handheld light box. I found one on eBay for a dollar and it arrived within the week.

Peering through to the small bright screen, I gazed at two pretty blond girls standing beside a young Uncle Manny. They were our cousins, Rachel and Lois, I knew, but I had no way of telling one from the other. The Manny of our childhood was a lonely divorcé, estranged from his girls.

"Maybe Bess will take me back someday," he often said with a sigh. But the one evening Aunt Bess joined him at our dinner table, she sat stiffly, as if she could barely stand having him so near.

In slide after slide, Mom wears beautiful clothes. A wide aquamarine skirt made fuller by layers of crinoline. A shapely Jackie Kennedy suit. Dressed to the nines, as she'd say, she does ordinary things. She bathes you in a freestanding baby tub. She sits on a park bench knitting something pink.

I learned that, in what must have been our parents' first

apartment together, they kept your crib beside their bureau, and that they dressed you in a bonnet for walks around town. In one photo, Dad kneels in the yard beside you at three or four, his arms all the way around you, as though you're the very thing that's holding him up.

I felt stunned by the sweetness of these images, especially the adoring way Mom gazed at you as a baby. Your troubles in the family really did begin with me, just as I'd always feared. You, our parents' adopted daughter, were well cared for and loved until their surprise flesh-and-blood child made you expendable. "They turned you against me, didn't they?" you had insisted all those years ago. But actually, it was me—my unexpected entrance into the family—who had turned them against you.

Putting away those damning slides, I returned to the photos of you from our old plastic bin. The puckish six-year-old. The aggrieved teen. The haunted, malnourished addict at twenty-one. And then, the one close-up I had of you and Dad side by side, the faded brick buildings in the background placing you at the Training School. Dropping onto the couch, I stared at your faces, focusing on the similarities. Round cheeks, sly half smile, full fleshy nose.

The paternity question had once been a kind of escape for me. A mystery to solve when I thought of you in those first years after your death. But now it felt like a lifeline. After all, if your birth had been both proof and consequence of Dad's infidelity, then Mom's rage, misplaced as it was, would make sense separate from me.

That photo of you and Dad lived on my desk for weeks. But the more I stared at it, the less I actually saw it, the way a word loses its meaning when repeated too many times. I wanted someone to think about this with me, someone deeply intuitive who could offer a fresh perspective.

One quiet afternoon at the library, I typed the words *psychic* and *photographs* into Google just to see what would come up. My screen filled with images. A woman, draped in scarves, staring into a crystal ball. A neon sign decorated with moons and stars. Finally, I found an article about a man named Jimmie Bay. Clients came to him with pictures of their love interests for relationship advice. He had a reputation for being spot on.

To prepare for our session, I scanned photos, had the slides digitized, and emailed all the images to Jimmie. On the morning of our appointment, I sat on the couch next to my overstuffed bookcase and propped my laptop and the receiver of the cordless phone on the coffee table. The first photo Jimmie and I looked at together was among the last ever taken of you. In it, you're next to Dad on the plaid couch in your Webster Street apartment. Between you, little Ray-Ray stares wide-eyed into the camera, his mouth open, as though he has something to say.

Jimmie had a warm, inviting demeanor and an easy laugh. At the start of our call, our conversation had been light and chatty. Now, he began to speak quickly. "Your sister had a very erratic life. A lot of twists and turns. Nothing was ever stable or secure. Abusive relationships, abusive family members. A lot of addictions around her. And she was a nomad. Never in one place too long."

Amazed, I stared at the photo. In it, you smile mildly for the camera, giving nothing away.

We turned to a photo of you as a child of six or seven.

"Wow," Jimmie said softly. "She started out as such a bright soul. I just feel she got lost along the way. Overlooked. There was some kind of abuse with her, with a family member. Something to push this in this direction."

I immediately thought of the dustpan beating. "Well, I'm aware there was some abuse from my mother. I witnessed ..."

Jimmie cut me off. "I know there was some sexual abuse with a male family member. That I can tell you."

I felt highly alert, my body pulsing as though all I had in my system was caffeine. But later, listening to the tape of our reading, I'd hear my voice slow down here, delaying whatever understanding I'd bring away with me. "You're sure it was family?"

"Yes. She got tainted very young. There were so many things that were ignored with this girl. So many signs."

Heart pounding, I directed Jimmie to the photo of you and Dad in Hudson. "You don't think he was the abuser, do you?"

"No. I don't get that vibe with him. I can see he ignored a lot of things with her and was extra hard on her. But I feel like the abuse came from an uncle."

"Not Uncle Manny?" I pictured our goofy uncle who called me monkey and spoke in malapropisms. "No," I decided aloud. "He was a sweet soul."

"As hard as your sister tried to fit in," Jimmie went on, "she could never find her place in the family. When she tried to tell your parents about the sexual abuse, they didn't know how to deal with it, so they blamed her and shut her out. That's when things started going downhill."

I was still jittery, but this distressing turn in our session also made me feel depleted. Meanwhile, my hour with Jimmie was going fast and I hadn't yet broached the question that had sent me to him in the first place. "Can we look at an earlier picture? I'm trying to find out something about Angie's birth, since she was adopted into my family."

We opened the photo where Dad kneels in the yard with little you in his arms.

"Did he adopt her from another family member or something?" Jimmie asked. "Because I feel like there was something family related there too."

"Is it him?" I blurted. "Is she his?"

"I need a picture where the eyes are clear."

"Let's go back to that other one, the file called, *With Dad in Hudson.*"

Silently, we each stared into two pairs of smiling brown eyes. "Yeah, I do feel like there's a bloodline here."

"Did my mother know?"

"Yes." We moved to a photo of you as an infant crawling toward Mom who smiles at your approach. "Your mom was aware of the pregnancy and the baby. She tried to love her and thought she could, but she had some type of mental issues with her. Also, she was stuck with a lot of responsibility. Your father didn't help a lot, and I feel like that contributed to her resentment."

I nodded, remembering Dad barking, "I'm not a babysitter," when we were small.

The last photo I had Jimmie look at was of the two of us. Steeling myself, I asked him if you saw what happened to you in our family as my fault.

"No, I don't see any blame. She loved you and she wished she could have stayed to build the bond with you. But she had to leave to protect herself. She also wanted to protect you from all the bad things in her life. She loved you," he repeated as my throat tightened. "And that love is still here."

When the session ended, I wandered around my apartment, from the lamp-lit living room to the bright kitchen where the open door to the terrace let in the sound of children playing in the courtyard below. I felt myself shaking, my right arm pulled tight against my chest. You'd been molested. Of course you had. Tina had told me as much. But given the other bombshell she'd thrown into that conversation, and my own lifelong habit of sealing myself off from your impossible life, I'd never really taken it in. Now, finally,

I could see how the abuse had shaped you. I recalled the morning you leaned over me when we were both still little, saying, "Kiss me" in the commanding tone of a lover. I thought of how fascinated by sex you'd always been. Your obsession, I'd assumed, had come from within, a result of hormones and your mysterious genetics. Was that how our parents explained it? Not exactly, but I'd witnessed Mom's fights with you. I heard the accusations she tossed your way.

I clearly remembered Tina telling me it happened with a neighbor. But Jimmie Bay seemed certain the abuser was someone in the family, and I couldn't simply dismiss that after everything he'd said that I knew to be right. Had you altered the facts out of embarrassment when you confided in our half-sister? Or was the perpetrator someone you felt the need to protect?

When Manny died, Dad discovered that he had mounted childhood pictures of the two of us on cardboard and propped them on his dresser. It was a detail Dad found touching. Remembering what little girls we were in those photos, I clung to that detail, as if it proved there were lines Manny never would have thought to cross.

Still, Jimmie believed it had been an uncle. Of our uncles, only Manny ever came to see us. I could still see his pained expression when he asked if I'd said something to hurt you. Had he been hurting you through it all?

"You didn't say something mean to hurt your sister, did you?" You were so rarely home by then. I remember wondering when and where you would have spoken to him.

I opened my yellowed copy of a 1971 paperback called *Runaways* by Lillian Ambrosino. Among the many sentences I'd underlined in its earliest chapters was this: "The easiest recourse [for runaways] is to turn to a friend or relative..."

That was certainly true once you made your way to California. But had it started before that? When you first ran away, did you show up on Manny's doorstep? A pretty girl, lonely and desperate for affection? An irresistible gift?

My old friend Natalie and I had recently reconnected through Facebook, and I'd asked her what she remembered about you. She sent this response: "I have one really vivid memory. We were in 104 Park on the benches near the sandbox. That is where Andra told you & me & a couple of other girls how babies were made. You know- the mechanics... :). We were so shocked, but very interested. I remember thinking that I could never get married because I could never do that. So funny & very Andra!"

Through another childhood friend, I found a classmate of yours from sixth grade. She wrote in an email that she remembered you "...strutting around in high platform shoes and exuding a certain kind of either aloofness or maybe arrogance or maybe it was just insecurity." She told me you didn't have many girlfriends. "If she was hanging with anyone she was hanging with the boys!"

I tracked down one of those boys, your grade school crush, and met with him in his Manhattan office. There, surrounded by tall filing cabinets, large drafting tables, and a desk piled with papers, I learned that you weren't exactly well-liked by the guys either.

"Andra was alone all the time," he recalled. "I'd see her drifting around the playground in the afternoons like she had nowhere to be."

"Everybody loves Andra," Mom used to say. I hadn't realized how tightly I'd held to her assertion until that moment when I learned it wasn't actually true.

Day after day, you wandered the playground, though it was the boys' turf, lingering on the edges, watching as they played their impromptu games.

"Hey, Gritz," they taunted. "Bet those boobs of yours aren't real."

"Yes, they are," you insisted.

"Prove it!" they called back. A dare.

The first few times, you refused. "I don't have to prove anything. I know what's real." But one afternoon, you followed the group of seven or eight boys to an enclosed structure in the park. Angie, do you hate that I know this? I kind of hate that I do.

"She'd only go if I went too," your old classmate admitted. "While I was a part of it, in a strange way, I was also her protector. I think she had a sense that nothing really bad would happen as long as I was there."

Insisting he go first, you lifted your shirt, pushed your bra out of the way, and stood still while the boys took turns wiping their palms on your breasts.

"She had a craving need for attention," Jimmie Bay had said. And for those few minutes on a long afternoon, you had attention. You proved you were real. "Feels mother loves 'real' sister, not her," was written in your permanent record that same year.

The *breast test* happened again in a secluded spot by the bay. It never went further, just a seconds-long feel from each of the boys. Still, whenever they saw you, they now had a new way to greet you. "Whore, whore, we want more," they called.

Hearing this, my eyes stung. I thought of the other girls in your sixth-grade class who, like me, played under the watchful eyes of their parents and jumped rope to very different kinds of rhymes.

Another detail that soft-spoken man shared with me that afternoon was your not-so-secret code. "Whenever she got her period, she wore her red coat."

"She told you that?" What eleven-year-old girl advertises to boys when she's bleeding? I thought, but I knew the answer. A girl without a sense of boundaries. A victim of sexual abuse.

Chapter Twenty-One

For the remainder of my time in high school you were mostly out of touch, and one afternoon in my senior year, I decided to try to capture how it felt to have a runaway absentee sister. Staring across at your empty bed, I wrote the word *Abandoned* on top of a clean notebook page. From there, I described you as "...warm, and friendly and liked by everyone" and said that your "world of music, makeup, and boyfriends" fascinated me. "But," I went on, "I didn't understand her discontent with what was my security," and claimed that you had one fault: "...a thirst for freedom and the need to break the ties of family life."

This is what still exists from our all-too-brief time as sisters: the photos, the ring set, and, taking up a full page in the 1980 Far Rockaway High School yearbook, that flowery and vacuous essay in which I say, "I was vaguely aware of the hurt that she caused in my parents" and nothing about the many ways I witnessed them hurting you.

Sometime during the months I waited to see my essay in print, you finally called.

"I'm engaged, baby. This is it. I'm totally happy."

"Congratulations!" I sat down at the dinette table and propped my feet on the opposite chair, as though you weren't calling long distance. "Engaged to who?"

"His name is Ray. The first thing he said to me when we met

was, 'Marry me!'"

"Really?" I glanced up at Mom who hovered nearby, eaves-dropping. "What did you say?"

"I thought he was handing me a line, so I looked him up and down and said, 'Get me a ring.' And he did. The next day, he brought me one of those toy diamond rings we used to get out of gumball machines."

"That is so romantic!"

"Yup." I heard you mumble something with your hand over the receiver and realized you weren't alone.

"He's there?"

"Yeah, baby. He wants to talk to you."

This was a first. You had told me about plenty of boyfriends over the years, and even a few potential fiancés, but none had ever asked to speak to me.

"Ona! Baby sister," said a deep, friendly voice. "I've heard so much about you."

"Mostly good stuff?"

"A hundred percent. For one, Angie tells me you're an excellent student."

"Yeah, you know. She's the body, I'm the brains."

Ray's laugh was booming and real. "Stay in school, sweetheart. Don't be like me and your sister."

Ray retold the story of wanting to marry you the moment you met, then asked me what music and TV shows I liked. After we talked awhile, Mom cleared her throat, letting me know she wanted a turn.

"My mom would like to meet you too," I said.

Was it naïveté that allowed me to believe she'd simply introduce herself and congratulate you both? Willful ignorance? Somehow, just as I'd meant it when I wrote that I didn't understand why you were discontented at home, I believed she'd be glad to hear you sounding so happy. Even now, given that your happiness was three thousand miles away and would cost her nothing, I don't know why she couldn't just let it be.

"Before you marry my daughter, you should know what you're getting yourself into," she started.

"Ma, don't!" I reached for the phone, but she held it tightly and waved me away.

"You know, everybody loves Andra, but you can't always trust her. She's very good at telling people what they want to hear."

Her back to me, she told Ray that you had once helped rob your old boyfriend, then described the time you'd stolen my jeans and disappeared. I paced around the kitchen, as helpless as I'd been as a five-year-old watching that dustpan come down on your legs. Finally, I heard, "Well, it's all true. He has a right to know," and knew you were back on the line.

"Let me speak to her," I demanded, and this time Mom acquiesced. I waited until she left the room, dust rag in hand. "Angie? You okay?"

"Why would she say those things? Why would she do that?" Your voice sounded so deflated and shaken, I had to close my eyes to bear it.

"I'm so sorry," I said, trying to swat away the familiar feeling that Mom's actions were my doing. If she was a part of me, as I believed her to be in those moments, she was like my right, palsied side. My brain sent messages, but something went awry on the receiving end. "I'm sure she didn't mean it," I said, willing my words, hollow as they were, to erase the memory of hers.

But, Angie, I probably stayed mad at her for all of an hour. When I came out of my room, I smelled my favorite dinner, turkey breast and sweet potatoes, roasting in the oven. After we ate, Mom and I sat together in the TV area reading our books like we always did, and then watched *The Love Boat* or *Soap* while Dad watched *Hawaii Five-O* in the other room. I'd be starting college in just a few months and, though some of my friends would stay home and attend Queens College or Hofstra, Dad had talked to me about the importance of going away to school. He said I was too dependent on Mom, and I knew he was right. You'd fended for yourself out in the world by the time you were twelve, yet here I was, seventeen, and Mom still rushed to prepare a snack for me the moment I so much as wandered toward the kitchen. At the core of this was my disability, though she never said it. "There's nothing you can't do," she'd assure me, but what felt like a moment later, she'd insist, "Let me do that for you." Mom still cut up my meat and she trimmed my finger and toenails for me. She even tied my shoelaces since she didn't think I made them tight enough.

"Mom! I'm not a baby, you know," I'd complain, rolling my eyes while she fussed over me, annoyed and also ashamed. To be babied, I understood, was to be loved too much. To be given not just my share of our mother's devotion, but also yours and our half-siblings'. Yet, though I grasped this, I never lingered there long. Because, of course, I wouldn't have traded. Because, of course, I loved her too much too.

Chapter Twenty-Two

With all the rifts in our family, I had no idea how to go about finding Manny's daughters, Rachel and Lois. There was a Lois Gritz on Facebook, but I quickly realized from her photos that she was much too young to be our cousin. I didn't have any luck with *whitepages.com* either. It seemed likely they'd both married and changed their names.

When I rooted around in my desk for Mom's worn address book, I expected it to be one more dead end. But under an entry for a Rachel and Nick Wiseman, Mom had written "Lenny's niece" in parentheses. The frayed little book was decades old, so I wasn't prepared when the man who answered the phone turned out to be Rachel's husband.

"And you are?"

"A cousin of Rachel's?" Oddly, as I said this, it felt like a fib.

"Honey..." Nick called.

A moment later, a woman came on the line. "Yes?"

"Um, hi." This was happening so fast. I wasn't sure how to begin. "My name is Ona Gritz. I think we're cousins?"

"We sure are! Wow. I can't believe you're calling me. I'm trying to think if we ever met."

"Maybe when I was still a baby?"

"I don't know. I remember your sister really well, though."

"You do?" Not wanting to mishear a word, I closed the door against the piano concerto on Dan's stereo and the occasional text message ding from Ethan's phone.

"Yeah. I remember when Andrea was first adopted, and also when she was about preschool age."

It felt dizzying to speak with someone who knew you in that small six-year window before I did.

"Do you mind telling me what you recall?"

"Well, for one thing, I always worried about Andrea. It didn't surprise me, how things ended for her."

"So, you heard."

"Sure. Your father phoned my mother as soon as he learned about it."

"Huh." Once again, I was struck by how little I knew about our family. I had no idea Dad had kept in touch with Aunt Bess.

"Anyway, your sister always seemed kind of..." Rachel paused, searching for the right word.

"Wild?" I supplied, the word our parents had always used for you.

"No, not wild. She seemed lost to me. I was only a kid, but even so, I could feel that there was something off about the way your parents treated her. Clearly, your mom hadn't been for the adoption. Andrea was just starved for attention, and she wasn't getting it. Not from your mom."

"What about my dad?" I paused. "I guess he wasn't very involved either."

"Not from what I remember. Your sister really troubled me. In fact, in college I studied child psychology and I wrote a paper about her. About the potential effects of your mother's disinterest. That's how big an impression the whole dynamic left on me."

I tried to imagine Mom acting indifferently to a lovely little baby. What would that even look like, I wondered. But, after a moment, I knew.

"If he annoys you, just push him down," you'd said to me about

Ray-Ray on the last full day of your lives. I'd felt appalled by that, but now I understood. You were merely passing on what you'd received.

Yet, there were also those early photos I'd recently discovered where Mom gazed at you tenderly. Maybe the answer was simple. Pictures lie. Perhaps not to someone with Jimmie Bay's powers, but they lie to the rest of us. "Your mom tried to love her and thought she could," Jimmie had said. Pictures capture an instant, a pose. They catch us pretending to be the kind of people we wish we were.

"There was one time Andrea was at our house," Rachel went on. "She had some toy and she tried to give it to my mom. Like she felt she had to give up something to get affection. My mom told her, 'No, that's yours. You don't have to give me anything for me to love you.'"

My God, I thought. Angie was primed for sexual abuse.

"Rachel, can I ask you about your dad? Was he..." How could I possibly phrase this? "Was he a good guy?"

The change in her tone was remarkable. "No. I wouldn't say that," she snapped.

While I was on the phone with Rachel, she gave me her younger sister's number. Lois also remembered you vividly and was eager to share what she knew.

"Your parents would come over, and your mother always tried to make me babysit. 'Go take Andra in the bedroom and play with her,' she'd say, like she couldn't wait to get rid of her. I hated that, but then my mom would rescue me. She'd say, 'Come out and visit with the company. It's not your job to watch her daughter.'"

"What was Andra like when you were alone together?" I asked, pressing the phone to my ear.

"All over the place. She insisted on wrestling. 'I want to fight,' she'd say, and bat at me with her little fists. I'd let her do it for a while, but if a grownup opened the door and peeked in, she'd stop and act all quiet. Finally, I asked her, 'Are you mad at me?' She shook her head, so I said, 'Well, why do you want to hit me?' and she said she didn't know."

Overly aggressive. Odd behavior. Those unexplained phrases from your school records rang in my ears hours after Lois and I hung up the phone. I thought of how rough you could sometimes be, pinning me to the floor and fanning your hair over my belly until the tickling turned painful enough to make me cry. But in my memory, those moments were rare. I can't even name a single time you'd actually said anything mean to me. How many kid sisters can say that?

Before Lois and I said goodbye, I asked if she'd stayed in touch with Dad's other niece, Lauren, his sister Ellen's daughter.

"I haven't seen her in years," she mused. She was able to tell me Lauren's last name, though, and I quickly found her online.

Like our other paternal cousins, Lauren seemed surprised but also pleased to hear from me. When I asked what she remembered about you, she described a visit to the winterized bungalow on Beach 27th Street where we'd lived until I was two. It was a blustery December afternoon, and she recalled Mom shooing you, at five years old, out of the house.

"Your mom liked to keep things clean," Lauren said, as though this might come as news to me. "Of course, kids get into messes. So, she made your sister go out, though clearly Andra didn't want to. It was a nasty day and, right on the beach like that, there was no one around for her to play with."

Mom's harshness toward you predated me. I had proof now, in triplicate. It wasn't my birth, or her overabundance of love for me, that had made it so. I waited to feel a flood of relief with this knowledge, but whatever comfort I took from it was fleeting.

Something had started to shift in how I thought about you.

Until then, even as I studied photos of you as a small child, the person I saw was my big sister, a girl who could handle anything. You might be strapped into a carriage, wearing a baby bonnet, and still the little face that peered from under the brim seemed mature to me, your eyes knowing.

But finally, these talks with our cousins began to change that. I now had moments when I looked at you in those early pictures and recognized your vulnerability and your trust. When I saw you through a mother's eyes.

I remembered a game Ethan had made up when he was six. The age you were when I was born. The age I was when you began running away. He called it Lost Boy, and he liked to play it as we walked home from his afterschool program.

"Pretend I'm a lost boy and you just found me crying on the sidewalk. Ask me where my parents are, and when I say I don't know, tell me that you've always wanted a boy just like me and you have a room for me with toys and clothes. Tell me you wish I was your little boy and that I can stay with you as long as I like, even if it's forever."

Ethan insisted on acting out this scenario again and again. Day after day, I said my lines, though I never understood how he came up with the game or why it was important. I simply figured it must be meeting some kind of need. Something innate in all of us, a need to be told, "I have always wanted someone like you. There is a place for you here." Maybe that's what the *Property of* stamp on your lower belly was all about. Not a branding, as I'd always thought, but a claiming. She's valuable and she's mine.

Meanwhile, I continued to learn more about the ways our parents neglected you.

"I haven't thought about any of this in ages," Lois called to say, days after our initial conversation. "But, you know, Grandma was very concerned about Andra."

"She was?"

"Sure. Andra was just a little girl, four or five, but your mom would let her run around the neighborhood all day. Grandma tried to talk to Aunt Edie about it, but she'd just say, 'Oh, she's fine. Everybody loves Andra.' Of course everybody loved Andra! They could do whatever they wanted to her."

"Right."

This brought me to the reason I'd sought out Manny's daughters to begin with.

"I know you weren't close to your dad..." I started carefully.

"He was awful," she spat.

"Awful how?" Rachel had told me that he'd been verbally abusive to Aunt Bess, but she wouldn't say much else.

"My dad was always screaming. He'd come home from work and right away start yelling at my mom, 'Where's my dinner?' As soon as we were grown enough, and she could land a good job, she got out of there."

"What was he like to you and Rachel?" I pressed.

"Cold, like he didn't know how to relate. 'Turn that music down,' he'd holler at us as soon as he was done yelling for his dinner."

"I never saw that side of him," I said quietly, recalling a time he'd marveled at the way I sang to the radio. "How do you remember all those words, monkey?" he'd wanted to know.

"Uncle Manny had a high fever as a child," Lauren explained when I called to talk to her about this. "That's why he didn't seem all that with it. The fever affected his brain."

With her, a fellow niece rather than a daughter, I let myself ask the question directly. "Do you think there's any chance he sexually abused my sister?" I left out that a psychic had suggested the possibility.

"Of course, there's no way to know," Lauren answered. "But one thing I do remember is that he had a problem with pornography."

"Huh." It certainly wasn't hard enough evidence to convict, but what grew clearer with each conversation was that I hadn't known our uncle very well at all.

One rainy Saturday afternoon, Lois and I met up in Manhattan. I was startled by how tiny our cousin was. She couldn't have weighed more than eighty-five pounds. Sharing one umbrella, we made our way to a crowded cafe in Times Square.

"You know, my dad always loved Andra. He talked about her all the time, saying what a great kid she was."

"That's nice to hear," I said, though what I thought of were her own words. "Of course everybody loved Andra. They could do whatever they wanted to her."

Lois pulled a napkin from the holder and tore it as she spoke. "The truth is, Ona, I have no good memories of my father. I was always afraid of him. Once, I was supposed to go somewhere by myself with him and I wouldn't do it. I went running back to my mom."

Hearing this, I leaned into the table. "There's something I've been wondering about your dad and my sister." I stopped. She appeared so small and frail, a thin winter branch in what looked like children's clothing.

"You can ask me anything, Ona. Really," she insisted.

I looked into her eyes, and she held my gaze with a steadiness that surprised me.

"Okay. Do you think he was capable of abusing her? Sexually?"

"No, I don't think so," she answered. "Well, I don't know. Maybe. There was something once. A neighbor complained that, while she was exercising in the courtyard, she caught him looking at her through binoculars. I don't recall the details. Anyway, I can tell you, he never went after me that way."

I didn't doubt that Lois was being honest with me, but I questioned whether her memory was honest with her. "I'm such a nervous person. I've always been," she told me more than once that afternoon. She also confided that she'd battled an eating disorder all her life.

"I was lucky to have the mother I did. My troubles stem from my father. He made it such a tense household to grow up in."

I never spoke to Rachel again. When I left her a voicemail a few weeks after our one conversation, I got this message in response:

"Hi Ona. This is Rachel's husband, Nick. This really has truly nothing to do with you, but Rachel had a really horrific childhood caused by her father, and she really can't deal with anything that causes her any reminder of him. So again, nothing to do with you, but could you please be understanding and try not to contact Rachel or her sister again? There are wounds that Rachel needs to keep from reopening..."

"Do *you* feel that way?" I immediately called Lois to ask.

"Not at all. I'm really glad you reached out to me. Nick is just being protective."

I liked Cousin Rachel. Generally, people liked me. I'd never been banned from contacting anyone before.

"Can you give me Rachel's cell number or email? I want to ask her if this is really coming from her, or if Nick just took it on himself to step in."

"The two of them share their cell phone and email," Lois told me. "Ona, I think you have to let this go for now."

Finally, I did. But I couldn't let go of the new picture I had of our uncle. A porn addict. A Peeping Tom. A father who had harmed his daughters enough, in one way or another, that, decades after his death, they were both still angry and afraid.

Chapter Twenty-Three

Maybe it's because Dad worked nights, and we had to tiptoe past his bedroom door in the afternoons so as not to wake him, but I can barely access any memories of you and Dad together from when we were small. I know he could be stern, and that our rowdiness and chatter used to make him nervous, but I also remember him as playful and accommodating. When I was six or so, he and I made up a game we called Picture where we'd pose in front of the dresser mirror for a ticking invisible camera, then both fall over when the ticking stopped. Had he indulged you in this way as well? It feels to me as though he hid behind an actual camera through much of our childhood, documenting a birthday party or a day trip, capturing a sunny afternoon in the backyard.

Where he comes alive for me in your story is in California, when Mom, Dad, and I flew out to celebrate your twenty-fourth birthday and your marriage to Ray.

"Your picture doesn't do you justice," Ray said as we stood in front of the trailer the two of you shared in South San Francisco.

Months earlier, thrilled to finally have an actual mailing address for you, I had sent a wallet-sized copy of my yearbook photo. My before picture, I'd begun thinking of it. Before I got my Diane Keaton perm and learned to use makeup. This visit was a kind of before too, my last trip in my last summer before leaving for college.

"Thanks," I said to Ray, blushing. I liked that broad shouldered, toughly handsome man whose hand kept finding your back pocket. Despite the rocky start with Mom, he seemed genuinely glad we were there.

"What do you think of the trailer?" you asked after our tour of the tiny yet surprisingly complete kitchen and no-nonsense bedroom with its curtain for a door.

"It's certainly efficient," Dad said. "I mean, really. For two people, what more do you need?"

That's when you and I exchanged glances. You hadn't yet told our parents, but, if all went well, in another six months you and Ray would grow into a family of three.

Soon, Dad's camera came out, and we began posing for pictures. You and Ray in the doorway of the trailer. The two of us lounging on a patch of grass. Dad between us, arms thrown up in surrender as we poked at his ribs.

I thought back to the week of Steve and Terri's wedding in Las Vegas. When Terri and I talked while she secretly smoked, she confided that she'd experimented with drugs and had left behind a trail of boyfriends when she decided to marry our half-brother. "I had quite a wild streak," she'd said, and it flashed through my mind that if she could settle down and live a calm happy life, maybe you could too. It had been a distant hope, but now, just over a year later, it was actually happening. I felt an unfamiliar lightness and realized that I had been scared for you all this time. It was only as the weight of that fear finally began to lift that I could allow myself to name it.

Mom isn't in those photos at the trailer. Was she simply hanging back, or had she spent the afternoon elsewhere? Tina and Howie had moved up north by then, so she wouldn't have been with them. Maybe she was with Tina's childhood friend Susan and her husband Eric. I know we all went to see them during that visit. It was in their cozy house in the East Bay that Dad sent us both into shocked fits of laughter.

We had been sitting around their kitchen table, making small talk.

"How's Tina?" Susan asked. Growing up, she'd lived in the same building as Mom during the few years she'd raised Tina on her own. The two girls played together often, and Susan's mom and ours used to share a babysitter and escape to the movies on weekends.

"She's fine," Mom told her. "They're living near Mendocino and they've just had a baby, Gracen Sarah. Their first girl."

"I heard the only way to make a living up there is to grow marijuana," Dad put in.

"Dad!" you and I spat in unison.

Mom flashed him a look before following Susan into another room so they could call Tina together. But Dad didn't let the subject go.

"You hear so much about the stuff. I have to admit, I'm curious."

Eric studied him, started to speak, then hesitated. Finally, he asked, "Curious enough to try it?"

"Sure, if you've got some lying around."

Eric brought out a neatly rolled joint and demonstrated for Dad how to hold in the smoke before exhaling.

"Is this really happening?" you asked me when Dad took a turn.

"Nah. I'm pretty sure we're dreaming."

"Hey!" Dad complained as you plucked the joint from his fingers.

"That's how it's done," you explained, passing it to Eric. "You share it."

Ray winked at me since we both knew it was pregnancy that

kept you from bringing it to your own lips. "No thanks," he said when Dad offered him a toke. "I'm your driver, remember?"

With the joint down to a nub, Dad began wiping invisible crumbs off his placemat.

"You don't have to do that," Eric told him.

Dad continued brushing the clean surface. "You don't know my wife," he said.

That's when we fell against each other laughing.

"Tell them about Ma's living room," you urged.

"We've got a museum at our house," Dad said. "No one's allowed in but the queen."

"Your father's not how I imagined him," Ray whispered.

"This isn't my dad," you told him. "It's an imposter."

"Definitely," I agreed, too caught up in the moment to wonder what had allowed for this change in our usually conservative and practical father. Only now do I understand that he must have felt as relieved as I did to see you building a life with someone as present and steady as Ray seemed to be. He could let his guard down for once. He could believe you were going to be okay.

Chapter Twenty-Four

Not long after I got that entreaty from Rachel's husband on my voicemail, I went to an event in the Rockaways with women I knew back in high school. There, I ran into Natalie's older sister, Kim. We hadn't seen each other in close to forty years.

"I always felt so bad for you kids," Kim shouted over the music in the crowded pub. "You had quite a time of it."

I studied her age-softened, yet startlingly familiar face. "How do you mean?"

"Well, first there was what happened to Lisa."

I nodded, relieved to know that someone, in what we had thought of as the adult world, understood how Lisa's death had shaken and shaped us little ones.

"Then there was all the grief your sister put your family through."

I froze at this, the story our parents presented to the world. The one I had, unbelievably to me now, internalized, obedient daughter that I'd always been.

"Her sexual exploits, her running away..." She trailed off, implying the list was endless.

"Andra didn't have a great home life," I interjected. "She had her reasons."

Kim just shook her head. "No parent should have to go through that."

I drifted away soon after, images our cousins had given me turning like pages in a flipbook in my mind: a preschooler roaming the neighborhood unattended. That same small girl ushered out of the house to play on a desolate winter street. There was a term I had come across in my readings about juvenile incarceration: *throwaways*. It struck me that every runaway was a throwaway first.

Can we let ourselves be loved by such a God? I'd written a few years earlier in a poem that was part of a series based on stories from the Hebrew Bible. Even though we'd been brought up with next to no religion, I became obsessed with those harsh narratives for a while, horrified by the brutality and favoritism the God of the chosen people is known for. *Can we let ourselves be loved by such a God?* I wrote, unaware, until my husband Dan suggested the possibility, that what I was actually grappling with were the injustices in the family you and I had grown up in. *Adonai Echad*, Hebrew for 'There is only one God,' the poem concludes. *What choice do we have?*

Another term, a psychological one, I'd recently learned was *splitting*. This is when someone—a mother for example—is unable to accept the layers and contradictions in human nature, so she simplifies the world into black and white. One daughter good, the other bad.

And yet, ironically, it is precisely because I am our mother's daughter that I couldn't merely pronounce judgment and close the case on our parents. Once, back when I was in sixth grade, I came home bruised and scared after kids from the Redfern projects hurled snow-covered rocks at a group of us waiting in line for the bus back to our neighborhood of Bayswater. "Why do they act like that?" I'd cried to Mom, expecting she'd make a fuss since I'd gotten hurt. Instead, she answered calmly.

"You don't know what their lives are like. They may not have enough food in the house. Maybe both their parents work and they're alone a lot. You just don't know."

It's impossible to reconcile that empathetic woman with the one who'd kept us neatly pinned to our assigned roles. She cast you as the black sheep, the bad seed. At the same time, she forgave me every slight and infraction, so I could remain the well-behaved girl she'd needed me to be. Yet, on that afternoon when I was eleven, I learned from Mom, who had learned from the biographies and autobiographies she loved to read, that everyone's story is complex. It was neither the first nor the last lesson in compassion she gave me. Do you remember how people used to confide in her? Friends, neighbors, strangers on trains and supermarket lines sensed something in her that encouraged them to reveal their secrets and confess their fears. Often, she'd come home and share their stories with me.

"Life is hard," she'd say as her needle moved rhythmically through the fine holes of a needlepoint canvas. I'd press close to her on the couch, watching the picture slowly fill with color and softness, all the while loving the softness she exuded in those moments, the sympathy and calm.

"I've had a hard life myself," she told me after that revelatory trip to San Francisco the week of your twenty-first birthday. With her former life no longer a secret, she began to fill in the details. Gene had cheated on her constantly. Had you known that? He didn't even attempt to protect her from it. One night, at a party, he disappeared for nearly an hour, and when he finally strolled out of the bathroom, an attractive and disheveled woman ambled out on his heels. The only way Mom could sue for divorce was to have Gene pose for incriminating photos with women and discuss his infidelity in court. By then, she was down to eighty-five pounds from the stress.

Mom told me she was at her happiest in the three years she raised Tina on her own. Nonetheless, she felt pressured to remarry.

After all, being a divorcée and single mother in the sanctimonious 1950's came with no small amount of shame. Mom went to work in a matchmaker's office, figuring it could be a good place to meet a potential husband. She was right. Dad came to that office and, rather than fill out the matchmaker's forms, he asked the petite dark-haired secretary on a date.

"He looks just like Gene," Grandma Sarah exclaimed upon meeting him. But I'm sure what drew Mom to Dad were the ways he differed from her ex. He was solid and practical. A homebody she must have felt she could trust. But when they began to discuss marriage, they hit a snag. Dad had no interest in becoming a stepfather.

"I want a family," he explained. "But Tina would always be thinking of her real father. That would bother me."

Here is where the story remained inscrutable to me, no matter how bright a light I shone on it or how direct a question I asked. "Why did you stay under those conditions?"

"Life is hard," Mom reminded me. "I wasn't a strong person. Tina cried for her father and brother. I thought she'd do better with them."

Dad hadn't wanted to be a stepfather. And Angie, maybe Tina told you all this, but it went beyond declining to raise her. Tina made yearly visits to New York during her childhood, staying with Grandma Sarah, and Mom's brother Yach and his family. But she wasn't allowed in Mom and Dad's house. The same was true of Steve. Do you remember the one time he visited us, when his son Blaine and I were preschool age? Mom later told me that Dad had been so furious that she'd agreed to let them come, he refused to buy food for the house that week.

Steve and Tina may have been adults by the time you and I learned who they were to us, but when Mom and Dad first met,

Steve was a ten-year-old boy and Tina was just seven. Why was Dad's heart closed so tightly against two small children?

"Maybe it was financial," Cousin Lauren suggested when she and I talked about this over dinner one evening.

Ever since our first phone call months earlier, Lauren and I spoke often. But the last time we met in person was at Grandma Ann's funeral, when I was twelve. My memory of that long-ago afternoon is a mere patchwork of images. The rust-colored corduroy jumper I wore. The field of headstones engraved in Hebrew. The startling sight of Dad in tears. With both their parents gone, Dad and Lauren's mother had no reason to stay in touch. I never knew why they were so angry at each other, but the air between Dad and his sister was as icy as ever on that last sad day.

But now Lauren and I were reconnecting and working together to make sense of the past. As I sat across from her at a small oval table in a trendy downtown restaurant, I realized she looked like a slimmer, stylish version of Grandma Ann.

"Kids are expensive," she went on. "And while Uncle Lenny wasn't poor, he was famously stingy."

"That's true," I admitted. Dad had always seemed convinced that most people, including our half-brother and sister, wanted to take advantage of him. The little monetary help Mom gave Steve and Tina through the years, she managed on her own.

"Like when it came time to put Grandma Ann in a home," Lauren continued. "Your dad picked the most depressing, state-run place. I felt terrible seeing her there."

I thought of you, of course, locked up in Spofford and the Training School instead of one of the more benign Jewish residential centers. And then I thought of Dad, who had actually made a similar choice for himself.

"When he was about to have surgery for his brain cancer," I

told Lauren, "I asked him what he wanted to do afterwards. If he stayed at home, or with me, we'd have to bring in nurses, and he wouldn't spend the money. He insisted he only wanted to go to a place run by the V.A., which would be free."

I recalled how Dad always picked pennies off the street and rescued broken umbrellas from trash cans, bringing them home to stitch and bend back into shape. "I think he had a lot of insecurity from growing up during the depression," I explained. "It wasn't selfishness so much as fear."

That night, Lauren shared a troubling story involving the lower east side bar that was our family business from the 1950's through the early 1960's. Dad had opened it with Grandpa, and, Lauren told me, they also invited her father to join them in the venture. Soon after the E&G Bar and Grill opened its doors, Lauren's father began to notice that money went missing on a regular basis. He'd catch Dad and Grandpa pocketing cash from the safe or selling drinks without bothering to ring them up.

"But it was their own business," I said, confused. "They were stealing from themselves?"

Lauren was silent until I got it. By stealing from the business they'd asked Lauren's father to invest in, they were stealing from him. I felt a wave of guilt and decided right then to treat our cousin to dinner. Part of me felt like I should pay for all her meals for the rest of her life.

"Was Uncle Manny involved?" I asked.

"He was, but he didn't really have his own mind. I'm sure he was just a gopher."

As disturbed as I was to learn Dad's part in this, what really got to me was Grandpa's role. When he stole from his son-in-law, he was taking from his own daughter and granddaughter. How could he not have seen that? Moreover, as the parent, it was up to him to not just teach good values, but to model them.

You had known Grandpa Oscar briefly, of course, but he'd died while Mom was still pregnant with me, bequeathing me the O from his name. *Which*, I'd written in a poem, *like its thinner twin zero, is merely a hole / where he could have been.* I meant it as a love poem, having decided I liked him because he looked kind in photos. But it was a love poem to a stranger. A hole I could fill with whatever ideas I chose.

Our food arrived and I barely tasted it as I worked to take in this latest distressing detail from our family's past.

"Maybe it was Grandpa who first rejected Steve and Tina." The pieces clicked into place as I said this. Lauren's father had been an in-law, his link to our family through marriage rather than blood. If Oscar saw an in-law as other, someone outside the insular world he and his sons inhabited, he surely would have shunted stepchildren to the outside too. "Maybe he laid out the conditions under which he'd allow my parents to marry."

"I'd believe it," Lauren said. "Lenny definitely listened to him."

"But what about Grandma?" I asked. "Would she have gone along with it?"

"I doubt she saw herself as having any say."

Later, as I walked in the dark toward my train, I felt an immense weight pressing down on me. Made almost entirely of questions, it somehow grew heavier with every answer I got. I wanted to believe that, had Dad been less under his own father's control, he would have claimed Mom's children as his own. But, of course, by the time he and Mom met, he wasn't merely obeying Grandpa's wishes. He'd grown into the person Oscar had taught him to be.

Still, I felt keenly aware of the sorrows each of our parents had carried into their marriage. Dad had wanted to be a lawyer, but Grandpa needed his help in the business, so he had to leave college after only one year. Then there was Mom's heartache over Gene's affairs and what I had to assume was a devastating choice to disavow her children. Less than a year after their wedding, Peter was born and died in a blink. Eighteen months later, they adopted you, which struck me, in that moment, as a genuine act of hope.

There, on Sixth Avenue, I paused, causing a man walking behind me to step on the heel of my shoe. It hit me that the bar Lauren and I had been talking about all night was where Dad and your birthmother met. You were his daughter, I thought, more certain than ever. There was no way Grandpa Oscar's son would have brought home a child of strangers.

Chapter Twenty-Five

Angie, what can I say about Dad's and my trip to see you and Ray during my winter break freshman year, except that, before we left the restaurant on that first night, I really wish I'd stopped to pee.

"You're not pregnant too, are you, baby?" I remember you teased as we wandered that rundown patch south of Market in search of a bathroom. Finding no better options, we ducked into the Greyhound Station where I raced to the women's room and whispered "thank you" as I hovered over the dirty seat.

"Better?" Dad asked after I found you all huddled together on one of the few benches that didn't hold a sleeping drunk or mumbling addict.

"Much."

"Good," Ray said. "Let's get out of here."

As we headed to the exit, the men walked slightly ahead, and I couldn't help chuckling at how Ray dwarfed our 5'3" stoop-shouldered dad.

"Mutt and Jeff," I whispered, and you laughed.

We came so close to slipping out the door Ray held open and having the simple visit we'd planned.

"Where do you think you're going, Angie?"

The voice belonged to someone pleased with himself and entertained by the coincidence. I turned, expecting a round of awkward introductions. Ray shaking the hand of one of your old boyfriends, the guy acting shocked and impressed by your beach ball of a belly. Instead, that cocky uniformed police officer began reading you your rights.

"What's going on?" Dad broke in.

"What's going on is this young lady didn't show up for a court appearance on a drug charge," the cop said, giving you a smug little smile. "Isn't that right, Angie?"

"I cleared that up," I remember you telling him, but he just talked over you, continuing his recitation where he left off.

"You have the right to an attorney. If you can't afford one..."

Ignoring him, you looked to Dad. "It was my seizure meds," you explained. "They come in this huge prescription bottle I hate carrying around, so I had them in a sandwich bag. I already told that to the cop who decided to confiscate it from me." You searched Dad's face, as though, by believing you, he could fix this. "I cleared it up," you said again, turning to the officer. "You're making a mistake."

"All I know is there's an outstanding warrant."

"Is this a joke?" I asked as he stepped behind you, clipped handcuffs onto your wrists, then guided you toward an empty bench. Dad, Ray, and I followed. "It isn't funny. Not even a little." I kept prattling, though I meant to keep quiet. "I can't believe this is happening..."

When the officer left us to call in the arrest, I looked at Ray to see if he thought we should all try to bolt, despite your handcuffs. He stayed seated between us, one hand draped over my shoulders, the other on your knee.

"I'm sorry, Daddy," you said, though clearly I was the one who should apologize for dragging us into the godforsaken station.

"The guy's a jerk," I said.

"It's not legal," Ray told us. "Handcuffing a pregnant woman like that with her hands behind her."

I glanced across him at you sitting so far forward to make room for your bound hands, I worried you'd topple. "You okay?"

You shrugged and rolled your eyes.

"Well, we're just gonna have to hang tight," the officer came back to tell us. "I'm expecting a return call from the station. Then we can move forward."

"This isn't right," Dad said.

But the guy just checked his watch and plopped down next to him, as if we were all simply waiting to board the same bus.

"It's not right," Dad said again. "The kid's on medication. That's not a crime."

"We'll see about that," the cop answered, lacing his hands behind his head. "It's not her first offense, you know."

"We'll see about that," I mimicked under my breath. He was such a cliché, a stock character in a ridiculous scene from a terrible movie. That's exactly what this was, I thought, a hokey old film. Except I couldn't change the channel or turn it off.

Fear and rage are close-knit cousins, I learned that night. When the cop stood and moved languidly across the room to the window, I found myself trailing him, though my legs jelly-wobbled as I walked.

"That's not legal, what you just did," I heard myself say. "Handcuffing a pregnant woman behind her back. You're the one who's going to be in trouble when this is over."

He stared, appearing calm but for the way his nostrils flared. Then he began to scream. "You're an idiot. You don't know anything. You don't know a fucking thing."

For a moment, I thought he might hit me. Instead, he stormed out of the station. All the more shaken, I watched through the glass as he leaned into his car to pull out the radio on its stretchy cord and speak into it. Before long the image blurred, my old habit of crying whenever I got yelled at taking hold.

Stop this, I silently pleaded. Let us go. One prayer to the god of ludicrous situations, one to the suppressor of teenage sass. Help me stop making this worse.

Snuffling, I took a seat next to Dad.

"What's wrong, O.? What just happened?"

The sobs started as I admitted how the cop had ranted, calling me an idiot. "I am an idiot," I moaned. "And I'm so sorry I got us into this."

"All you did was have to pee," you were kind enough to say.

As Dad held me and patted my back, it almost felt like we'd be okay. That I just needed this good cry before we could walk out the door and continue our evening. But then our captor returned, and Dad leapt up, pulling his own small bottle of pills from his breast pocket.

"Here! You want to make another illegal arrest, you son of a bitch?" he fumed, shaking his medicine in the cop's face.

Remember how quickly the guy had his hand at Dad's throat? "You don't know what you're doing," he snarled. "You don't know who you're dealing with."

"Stop," I shouted, jumping to my feet.

But he held on, muttering threats and tightening his fingers on our daddy's neck.

"Come on, man," Ray said in his reasonable way. "Let the old guy go."

He *is* old, I thought as I stood there, helpless. He's sixty-two and he's going to die right here, choked to death in front of us.

"Stop," I wailed again.

Reluctantly, the cop released Dad, but only to snap handcuffs on him too. After that, there was the ride to the station, though I can't recall whether Ray and I squeezed into the patrol car with you and Dad or got there on our own. Too soon, our party was severed in half, bail set at $5,000 or $500 coupled with the deed to a house.

In the hotel room that became our think tank for the next few hours, I sat cross-legged on one of the beds while Ray stretched out on the other.

"Do you have $500?" I asked.

Ray stared at the ceiling, as though the solution to our troubles would appear in the plaster if he concentrated hard enough. "Yeah, that I can come up with."

"Well, I'll just call my mom and tell her she needs to wire us the deed to our house."

"It has to be property in California."

"It does? Shit."

"Got that right," he said.

"What if she goes into labor?" I worried aloud.

"Could happen." Ray sighed. "What about your other sister? Don't they have a house somewhere up north?"

"They're really poor. I'm sure they rent it."

Defeated, we fell silent. Ray turned out the light and I sat there, haunted by the image of Dad being choked. Again, I saw how his eyes grew wide, watched him swallow once, then set his fleshy chin firm against the assault. I wondered what he was doing right now. All I knew of jail I'd learned from the cop shows he liked to watch. Meanwhile, you were trapped in another bleak cell. I imagined your long fingers wrapped around the bars, knuckles whitening as you tightened your grasp with each contraction. What would happen, I fretted, if you really did go into labor?

Figuring I could think more clearly if I rested a while, I lay down and willed myself back to our last amazingly ordinary visit when your pregnancy was still a sweet secret you'd only shared with Ray and me. I recalled hamming it up for the camera in front of your trailer, and how funny Dad had been when he'd gotten stoned at Susan and Eric's lovely home across the bay.

"Ray," I burst, bolting upright. "I know who we can ask."

I didn't have Susan's number and couldn't even come up with her last name. We had to call Mom, but Ray convinced me to wait until morning, so as not to alarm her. In fact, he felt we shouldn't trouble her with what was going on at all.

"We thought we'd see if Susan and Eric could meet us for brunch," I finally told her, having rehearsed with Ray. "We've got nothing else planned for today."

"What a nice idea." The familiar sound of Mom's voice nearly undid me. "How is everything?"

"Great. Angie's about ready to pop. So, um...can I have their number?"

She laid the phone down to find her address book, and I glanced at Ray who nodded encouragingly.

"Let's see now," Mom murmured, back on the line. I heard the riffling of pages. "Ah, here we are." She gave me the number, then asked to talk to Dad.

"Everyone's waiting in the car," I told her, earning a thumbs up from Ray.

Thankfully, Eric answered on the first ring. "That's a lot to ask of someone," he said, after my rushed account of the nightmare we found ourselves in. Still, he met us at the courthouse, deed in hand.

It seemed like hours of waiting and filling out forms before you were returned to us, cursing and, just as we'd feared, in labor. Dad wasn't in great shape either with his new worrisome tremor, small but constant nods of his head.

Naturally, he was surprised to see Eric.

"He's our hero," I explained, which made both men blush.

After Dad's embarrassed thank you, Eric quickly left. The rest of us piled into Ray's car and headed to the hospital.

"Was it awful?" I asked.

Dad answered first. "I lied and said I had angina, so they put me in a cell by myself and were careful with me."

"Smart move," Ray said.

"Well, no one was careful with me," you informed us. "When I said I felt labor pains, they acted like I was faking. That bitch of a guard wouldn't even give me a Tylenol. I wish I'd had the baby right there so I could sue."

"It's better this way, honey," Ray said, unruffled as always.

Soon, Dad and I were left in a waiting room with posters of plump babies on the walls and piles of outdated magazines on the tables.

I squeezed close to him, awed by and grateful for how he'd stood up, not just for me, but for both of us against that terrifying cop.

"So, it wasn't too bad?" I asked again.

"Well, I wouldn't say it was the best night I ever had," he said, his head still nodding, as though agreeing with every thought that crossed his mind.

"What happens next? With the arrest, I mean."

"I call a lawyer when we get home and get the charges dropped."

"Will that asshole cop be in trouble?"

Dad snorted. "Probably get a slap on the wrist."

I laid my head on his shoulder and dozed for a while.

Finally, Ray appeared in the doorway, wearing scrubs and the goofiest of grins.

"Hey, Grandpa, Auntie. Come meet my son."

The first time I saw Ray-Ray, sleeping in your arms, I marveled at his good head of sandy blond hair and round cheeks. Studying his face, I decided he looked like a philosopher with a bit of bruiser mixed in. While we admired him, a nurse appeared with papers for you to fill out. You passed the baby to Dad and, as you did, he and I both caught sight of his extra toe. Dad quickly covered Ray-Ray's legs with a receiving blanket so you wouldn't see.

"She's got enough to think about right now," he whispered, and I felt struck by how rare it was, and how right, for him to protect you like that. It also flashed through my mind that, despite where you'd just spent the night, I'd never thought of you as someone in need of protection.

"Put the child's name right here," the nurse instructed.

"Raymond Martain Boggs III," you wrote in your loopy script. I noticed that you'd misspelled his middle name, but, following Dad's lead, I kept quiet about it.

You were asleep when the nurse came back to tell Dad and me visiting hours were over. "I'll take this little guy over to the nursery," she said, lifting the baby from Ray's arms.

"So, hey, congratulations." I squeezed Ray close.

Awkwardly, he and Dad went from shaking hands to a pat-each-other-on-the-back kind of hug.

"Thanks," Dad told Ray, reddening as he had when he'd said it to Eric. It made me realize he generally never needed help from anyone.

With our arms around each other, Dad and I paused at the nursery to peek at Ray-Ray through the plate glass window. Our sandy-haired charmer slept front row center amid his swaddled peers.

Nodding and nodding, Dad gazed at his grandson.

"This is worth everything we went through," he said.

Chapter Twenty-Six

No way our father would have brought home a child of strangers, I had thought after my dinner with Cousin Lauren. Seeking further proof, I sent away for your birth certificate and went to the research branch of the New York Public Library to learn the name you were given at birth.

Years before, as a new NYPL recruit, I'd taken a tour of the underground stacks in that stately building on Fifth Avenue. Beneath the polished floors where the public walked were miles of meticulously catalogued books. Like family secrets, I'd thought as I gazed at row upon row of neat spines. Except the information contained on those hidden shelves was available to anyone who asked.

I entered the Millstein Division and recognized the librarian on duty as the man who, weeks earlier, explained to me that if I had a copy of your amended birth certificate, I could match the number with your birth record and learn your original name.

"Amended?" I'd asked, digging in my bag for a pen.

"The one they make up when an adoption is finalized. It has the adopting family listed as the parents."

"What happens to the original?"

"It's locked away."

The following day, I'd gotten lost in a maze of damp side streets in lower Manhattan as I searched for the Department of Vital Statistics on Worth Street. Finally, I found it, just past Leonard Street, a small lane bearing Dad's name. When the certificate arrived in the mail, I studied Mom's signature, looking for some hint of the hesitation she must have felt before taking you into her life, but her handwriting was neat and sure.

Now, I pulled the two thick volumes marked 1956 off the shelf and lugged them to a table. My friend Julia was coming to help me search, so I placed one of the books in front of the empty chair across from mine. On top of that I laid an index card I brought to use as a straight edge, the crucial four-digit number—2483—written boldly in black ink.

All around, people typed on laptops or flipped through musty tomes. I settled in and studied the layout of the book. Three alphabetical columns with an initial for the borough and the certificate number next to each name. I'd learned from your birth certificate that you were born in Staten Island, known as Richmond, a gift since R's in the borough column were relatively rare.

I'd made it through six pages when Julia arrived. She sat down and opened the heavy book before her. "Exciting!" she mouthed.

Julia and I had been friends for nearly twenty years by then. She stayed at my apartment in the first weeks after her divorce. When my ten-year marriage to Richard ended soon after, Julia attended the hearing. She was also an emergency contact on Ethan's school forms.

"Should we call your family?" I once asked when I went to see her at a hospital after a medical scare.

"You're my family," she'd said. I'd always been good at finding sisters.

After an hour and a half, I was still in the A's, slowing down each time I came across a Staten Island baby, reading and rereading the entry. By the time I reached the B's, my back was stiff, my butt numb. Today I get to feel the aches for her, I thought, picturing you kneeling on the rough linoleum in our kitchen while I played on the floor nearby or sat at the table coloring. Once, Mom left us in the midst of your punishment to tend to the laundry. As soon as we were safely alone, you stood and rubbed your reddened knees.

"Don't tell, okay?" you said, taking the seat beside me for a moment. "It's just that it really hurts."

Had Mom expected me, a five-year-old, to act as a guard in her absence? "Want a cookie?" I asked, offering you the Lorna Doone in my sticky palm.

Bronx, Manhattan, Bronx, Manhattan, Manhattan, Manhattan, Kings. Finally, a Richmond. "I found her!" I heard myself blurt.

Julia came to my side of the table and read over my shoulder as I copied the spelling of your many-lettered name.

"Biancomano," I practiced saying aloud once we were out of the quiet library, enjoying the rounded sounds. "I am Andrea Biancomano's sister."

"I know Angie's birth name," I announced to Ethan, who'd recently started high school, when he got home that afternoon.

He dropped his heavy backpack on the floor. "Cool, what is it?"

"Biancomano."

He peered at the fat pillows of ravioli I had floating in a pasta pot. "Huh. Is that why we're having Italian?"

I remembered Dad asking about the first man I dated after my divorce, "Is he Jewish?" When I answered Italian, he gave me a playful, dismissive wave. "Eh, same thing."

Your birth family had always been an abstraction to me, a part of your story so out of reach, I felt free to fictionalize. In my manuscript *AWOL*, I'd made your mother a tough, raspy-voiced beauty like Lauren Bacall. But now she was an actual person with a name unusual enough that she could potentially be found.

Late that night, after Dan and Ethan had both gone to bed, I opened my laptop and looked up the name in *whitepages.com*. I hadn't put in a city or state, but the first Biancomano to come up was Pauline in Staten Island. She was eighty-six years old.

"I don't think it would be fair of you to contact Andra's mother," Cousin Lauren told me on the phone the next day. "She's an old woman who probably assumes her daughter has had a decent life and is alive and well right now. Is finding her really worth taking that away?"

I saw her point, but now that there was a real chance I might meet your mother, I couldn't let go of it.

"I'll be very thoughtful," I promised. "I'll choose my words carefully."

"Would you lie to her? Because if you tell her the truth about how Andra died, she'll be devastated."

For one crazed moment, I considered pretending to Pauline that I was her daughter, middle aged and thriving but for a mild limp. "Trust me," I said.

That weekend, I boarded an express bus to Staten Island and showed up unannounced at the senior housing project where Pauline Biancomano lived. A handyman let me slip into the lobby behind him. Moments later, I stood in an upstairs hallway that smelled of chicken soup and mothballs and knocked loudly on a painted metal door. After what felt like a long time, I heard the shuffling of feet and the click and slide of a heavy lock.

A tall woman with a deeply weathered face stood before me.

"Pauline Biancomano?"

"Yes?"

I couldn't help but stare. Where were you? Not in the eyes nor the shape of the mouth...

"I, um, came to see you because I believe we have a relative in common."

"A what?"

Raising my voice, I annunciated more slowly. "I think we share a relative."

Pauline shook her head. "I still don't understand what you're saying, but come in."

Just inside was a kitchen table. I sat down and glanced around. The small apartment was filled with heavy furniture, a once large home packed up and squeezed into these few rooms. Pauline sat beside me and waited.

"I've been doing some research on my family," I explained. "The reason I'm here is that I had a sister who was adopted."

"Adopted," Pauline repeated. "What a shame."

"She was born here in Staten Island. Her name was Andrea." I studied her face for a reaction, but she was simply listening. "Andrea Biancomano."

"Biancomano with an *o*? Because, you know, the name was originally Biancamano with an *a*, but my husband's people changed it."

"Your husband?" It had never occurred to me that she might have been married when she'd met Dad.

"They come from Salerno, his people," she continued. "If you're interested in the Biancomanos you can search their whole history on the computer these days. Salerno, Italy. Have you heard of a big Italian ship, the Conte Biancamano?"

"Yes! My sister's birthmother named her for the sister ship, the Andrea Doria," I reminded Pauline, watching her carefully. "It sunk the day before Andrea was born."

This seemed to hold no meaning for her. Finally, it came to me that I might have the wrong person. Still, I pressed on. "Can I show

160

you her picture?"

"She was adopted?" she asked, flipping through the small stack of photos I handed her. "Was she a happy child?"

"Yes," I answered, thinking you were, by nature.

"She looks a little like my daughter."

"Really? Can I see a photo?"

Pauline lumbered into another room. Alone at the cluttered table, I noticed a crumpled five-dollar bill. So trusting, I thought. Like Angie.

The framed photo Pauline handed me was of a dark-haired bride. She was beautiful, but she didn't especially resemble you.

"Everyone is interested in family these days," Pauline mused. "They call me when they have questions, so I sent away for information. You could do that too, find out about the Biancomanos going all the way back to Salerno."

"What I'm interested in right now is finding out about my sister."

Pauline squinted at the picture on top of the pile. "And she's where now?"

"She died young." I braced myself, but she asked nothing further.

"Such a shame," she said, "adopting away children. In my opinion, adoption should be illegal."

"Illegal?" Had she somehow confused adoption with the politically charged subject of abortion? No. She'd asked about your childhood. She was looking at photos. Pauline understood that you had been born and had lived in the world for a time.

She leaned toward me. "Are you a mother?"

"Yes, I am."

"Can you imagine giving up your child?"

"Well, no. But people have their reasons. Accidents happen."

"Accidents. Now, you know better than that. My mother taught me that if you don't want to have a baby, there's only one activity you need to avoid."

I thought of Mom then, who, as judgmental as she so often was with you, had matter-of-factly taken you for an abortion when you were sixteen. "She has to have something removed," she'd explained to me then. Years later, in my twenties, she did the same for me, bringing me to a clean doctor's office, paying the bill, consoling me afterwards while I cried.

Now, I stared at Pauline and knew for certain she wasn't your birthmother. She was that one disapproving aunt or cousin or sister-in-law everyone hid the family secrets from.

"I think it's a very good thing she didn't turn out to be Andra's mother," Lauren said when I called to relay what had happened.

"Probably so."

Nonetheless, I wrote emails, Facebook messages, and letters to all the Biancomanos I could find. There weren't many—maybe seventeen people all together—who spelled their name with an *o* at its center. One, a woman named Jacqueline, also lived in Staten Island, but would have been merely eleven when you were born. Pauline was the only Biancomano of an age to have given birth in 1956.

She also seemed to be the only Biancomano with a current address listed correctly online. Soon, my mailbox filled with envelopes stamped with red accusatory fingers and the words *address unknown*. In the end, that was the closest to a response I received, my own letter boomeranging back to me in multiples. All that came of my efforts was a lovely Latinate sound that sometimes ran through my head like a snippet of song. Andrea Biancomano. A.B. The initials you inadvertently reclaimed when you married Ray

Boggs and took his name.

As far as I know, you had never wanted to meet your birth-mother. It makes sense. You'd faced enough rejection and didn't need to go looking for more. Why then had I chased after Pauline so doggedly? I told myself I was looking for answers, as if learning of your beginnings could be a way to offer you a fresh start, just as I'd tried to do by writing a new ending for you in *AWOL*.

But, in truth, what I most wanted, when I believed Pauline to be your biological mother, was a mere hour in her presence. I wanted to hear her voice, see an expression cross her face, watch her gesture with her hands as she spoke. I even wanted the smell of her, as if her very existence, her pheromones, anything about her, might actually bring you back to me.

Chapter Twenty-Seven

Another estranged relative I reached out to in my quest to finally understand our complex and secretive family was Uncle Yach, Mom's only surviving sibling. I found a listing for him in Del Ray Beach, Florida, but I doubted he'd agree to talk to me. He had broken all ties with Mom before you and I were born. I knew she had made several attempts to reconcile through the years, but he'd always rebuffed her.

Early one evening, Dan away for work, Ethan at his dad's, I tried our uncle's number. Yach wouldn't come to the phone, but his wife Helen seemed genuinely pleased that I called.

"Tell me everything, darling. Do you have a happy life? Do you have children?"

It had been Dad who introduced Yach to Helen. Had you known that? She was an old girlfriend of his, and I'd always assumed that the rift between Mom and Yach had to do with the hurtful way Dad had broken up with her.

"No," Helen informed me now. "That wasn't it at all. Yach never got over that they sent Tina out west. He adored that little girl!"

Through Helen, I learned that Mom and Dad had put Tina on the plane just days before their wedding, leaving the impression that she'd only be gone the length of their honeymoon.

"A month went by, and I asked someone in the family when Tina was coming back. 'She's not,' they told me, and to tell you the truth, it scared me," Helen said. "A woman gives up her children and her parents say nothing about it? I thought, what kind of family am I getting myself involved with here?"

What kind of family. *Can we let ourselves be loved by such a God?*

"But you know, Ona. The more time I spent with Yach's parents, the more I understood your mother."

I leaned in, desperate to understand her too.

According to Helen, Yach, Mom, and their other siblings had been terribly neglected growing up. "I'm telling you, those kids weren't raised," she said. "They sprouted from the dirt like carrot tops."

The family had lived in an apartment at the back of Grandpa Sam's candy shop, and when the four kids came home from school, they'd find quarters waiting atop the register. They took the money and went to the movies, careful not to disturb their hardworking parents.

"No one checked on them as kids. Nobody cared whether they showed up at school, or if the boys went to their Hebrew classes. Sam was too busy, and Sarah was too furious to worry about anyone but herself."

"Why was she so angry?" I asked.

"She hated that Sam made her work."

I thought of you wandering our neighborhood as a little girl, our mother, like her own, too enraged to care.

"That's why I don't blame Edie for what she did to her children. She didn't have any role models. She wasn't taught. It's when she had you that she finally learned to be a mother."

"She was good to me," I agreed. Though, later, I thought it wasn't so much that Mom had learned to be a mother with me, but she'd finally chosen it. She allowed herself to love me completely.

After that first conversation, Aunt Helen and I grew close. I loved how forthright she was, how warm and fully engaged. Often, when we spoke on the phone, we found ourselves circling back to Mom's inexplicable decision to relinquish our half-siblings.

"Who came up with the idea?" I asked one night. "Did my mom offer to send Tina away, or did my dad bring it up? I know he told my mom he didn't want to be a stepfather..."

"That's right, he didn't. He definitely wanted children, but only his own."

Only his own. It struck me that, as Dad's ex-girlfriend, she might have a sense of how in character it would've been for him to have cheated on Mom.

"Helen, may I ask you something?"

"Anything, darling."

"It's about my other sister. Tina once told me she thought Andra was my dad's biological daughter."

Months earlier, I had raised the question with each of our cousins, but they hadn't even heard the rumor. I didn't expect Helen to know the answer either, but I thought we might speculate together. After all, I'd speculated with people about this for twenty-five years.

"What were you told growing up?" Helen asked.

"That she was adopted."

Helen sighed. "Okay, I'll tell you what happened."

In the pause that followed, I took a breath and held it. My hands trembled slightly, and I marveled at the wisdom of the body. How it recognizes a fissure, how it understands the enormity of whatever is on the other side.

"Andrea wasn't Edie's," Helen said, as though that too may have been in question. "But she *was* your dad's."

There. She'd said it. Now I knew. Had I always known? I couldn't be sure.

Of course, there was more to it, and I found I had to listen hard, the phone pressed against my ear, to hear Helen's words past the thrum of my own blood.

"Your parents had a baby who died. Did they tell you about that?"

I nodded. "Peter."

At three days old, our almost-brother died because of Mom's Rh-negative blood. She was missing an antigen, a protein most of us have on the surface of our red blood cells. The condition is hardly ever dangerous for a woman's firstborn child, but with each subsequent pregnancy, sensitized antibodies, those developed to fight off the baby's *foreign* Rh-positive cells, grow in strength and number. Essentially, Mom became allergic to the fetus and her immune system attacked. These days, the problem can be resolved by giving the expectant mother an injection. But not in Peter's time, nor mine.

In the story I'd grown up with, Mom's Rh-negative blood was part of what made me a miracle child. First, she was surprised that, at forty-two, she could get pregnant. Then, I was born frail, six weeks premature, weighing only five pounds. Because of the blood incompatibility that killed Peter, I required a full transfusion.

"We weren't sure you'd make it," Mom told me as she buckled my leg brace and tucked me in at night. The antibodies, the incubator, a dip in oxygen to the brain during the transfusion. Any of these may have caused my cerebral palsy. But the ritual telling of this story wasn't about disability. "You were my happy ending," Mom always said.

The tale opened with Peter—*Once upon a time a baby died*—and concluded with me—*and the little girl thrived.* I had always assumed you were outside of it, that your pages belonged in a different book. I was wrong.

Closing my eyes so nothing distracted me from Helen's words, I learned that, after Peter's death, the doctors told our parents Mom shouldn't get pregnant again.

"But Lenny wanted his own child. So, he found a woman and made arrangements."

"Arrangements," I repeated.

"You know, for her to be a surrogate."

"Oh." This possibility had never occurred to me, yet I found myself thinking, Of course.

"Your mother went along with it, but I can tell you, she wasn't happy about it."

"Oh."

After we hung up, I wandered to the kitchen to make a cup of tea, then drifted into the living room to gaze out the window at an anonymous rush of traffic while the tea grew cold. Taking a framed photo off the bookcase, I stared at the two girls in it. The teenager standing in her white miniskirt, smiling wryly. The seven-year-old kneeling on the grass between the V of her sister's parted legs. I caught myself looking for hints of resemblance. An old habit, this searching for clues, and it startled me to realize I didn't need to guess anymore. You and I were sisters in every sense of the word.

Angie, while I'd never imagined you to be a love child, I had thought you were likely the product of a reckless night. As it turned out, you were a decision.

It hit me that Dad must have been the one to name you after the Andrea Doria, the sunken sister ship to the Conte Biancamano. It matched his humor exactly. "I wanted to name you Hominy," he told me growing up, though I heard it as *Harmony*. "You'd be Hominy Gritz if your mom hadn't vetoed me."

"She vetoed me," he joked, but apparently Mom never had that power. In Dad's world, husbands had the final say. "I got married to have a family, so I'm going to do this," he must have pronounced. Or, "What's done is done. The baby is due in July, and I'm bringing it home."

"I understood your mother," Aunt Helen had told me the first time we spoke. "I don't blame Edie," she'd said. Now that I knew the fraught and thorny way you came into our family, I began to feel that I might understand her too.

"Your mom tried to love your sister, but she had some type of mental issues with her," the psychic Jimmie Bay had intuited. He also told me Mom had been aware of the pregnancy. At the time, that didn't make sense to me, but now I knew he was right.

In 1955, when you were conceived, few people would have had access to artificial insemination. For most, there was still just one way to make a baby. "Your uncle said your father and Angie's mother went at it one night behind the bar," Tina had claimed during that long-ago phone call. Meanwhile, Mom had ripped herself out of her first marriage because she found infidelity so painful. Now here she was, up against it yet again. I only wish Mom could have mustered whatever it took to give you the love, care, and attention every child needs. But, as it was, when she woke in the night to your crying, warmed your bottle, changed your diaper, the air around you must have felt charged with Dad's betrayal. Amplifying that hurt were her own young children on the other side of the country who weren't welcome in his house. I also think that, as you grew, your voluptuousness and sexuality came to represent your birthmother to Mom, which is why it so often ignited her wrath. Through you, she saw what that woman likely had that she didn't. By contrast, I not only came from Mom and inherited her less remarkable body, but was a broken thing—my vulnerability, my need to be nurtured, impossible to ignore.

"Your dad wasn't that way," Mom had answered when I'd asked

whether she thought you might have been his biological daughter. But, late in her life, she confided in me that he had upset her during her pregnancy with me by insinuating that he was having an affair. She secretly believed it was this, rather than the more scientific explanations the doctors offered, that caused my disability.

"You don't know where I go. You don't know what I do," Dad had blustered, stoking her insecurities until she folded inside where I floated, forming.

For days after talking with Helen, I felt furious at Dad. He was another Henry the Eighth, I seethed. Lopping off the heads of women who failed at producing an heir. Part of me was also cross with myself, though, for once, it wasn't for decisions that had been made before my birth. It was because, while it was clear to me that Dad should never have done what he did, and that your short life had been riddled with heartache and pain, I couldn't help feeling grateful to have entered the world with you as my fiercely loving and mischievous guide.

Meanwhile, as easy as it was to vilify Dad, I couldn't sustain it.

"One day, after I get married," he used to say to Cousin Lois when she was small, "I'm going to have a nice little girl just like you."

Yet, as badly as Dad wanted children, he was raised to be someone incapable of accepting a ready-made family. Someone who could never adopt anyone's child but his own.

Dad took countless photographs of you crawling around in your bulbous diaper, smiling peevishly as you emptied the contents of a tissue box, standing in the crib our parents kept in their room. This was part of how Dad showed affection, by slipping behind the camera, creating mementos that only captured the sweet side of his vehement desire to father a child. But there was still the heart-wrenching fact that his wife could barely get herself to look at his daughter. That when she did, the resentment she couldn't risk showing to him became the ice you saw in her eyes.

As much as I'd come to learn about you by this point, I was still left with questions. For one, where were you for the first sixth months of your life? Why didn't our parents bring you home right away? Did they worry that, like a nursing puppy, you were too young to be taken from your mother? Or is it possible our parents tried to renege, that Mom's desperation and ire got through to Dad and he agreed to call off his plan? Jimmie Bay had said you were essentially left on a doorstep. "Here, you deal with this. I can't deal with this. I want no part." Maybe Miss Biancomano, whoever she was, attempted to care for the baby she'd never intended to keep and couldn't really afford, and, after six months, insisted Dad stay true to his word.

One morning, while washing my face, I recalled that, when I was sixteen or so, a boy I didn't know had come up to me at a party to tell me he remembered you. As we stood together sipping our Cokes, he'd explained that you had dated his older brother.

"Wait," I'd asked after a moment. "How did you know who I was? That she was my sister?"

The boy seemed startled by the question. "Well, you look like her."

"That's funny," I said. "She's adopted."

He stared at me, plainly confused. It had confused me too, but I quickly buried the feeling under how much I loved the thought of resembling my pretty sister. Clearly, just as I had in regard to Tina and Steve, I'd collaborated with Mom and Dad in hiding the truth from myself about you.

Now, gazing at my face in the mirror, I saw that, while you and I didn't share as strong a likeness as Tina and I once did, our mouths were a bit similar. Lifting my hair, thick and wavy as yours,

I studied my slightly oversized ears like those I'd recently noticed in a photo of you. Finally, softening my gaze, I caught a quick glimpse of something subtle, something beneath the skin. Some essence of you that I'd recently stalked an eighty-six-year-old stranger in Staten Island to find.

Chapter Twenty-Eight

Now that I had an understanding of the beginning of your story, I knew it was time to start working my way back to the end. My first small step in that direction was to call our brother-in-law Howie and ask what he remembered about your early days in San Francisco.

"Angie stayed with us for a while when we lived in the Haight," he told me, and I recalled that to be in Haight-Ashbury in 1977 was to set the clock back ten years. The streets still flush with music, freedom, and tie-dye. It must have felt dizzying to you, at twenty, to find yourself in a place where no one eyed you with disapproval. A place where, it turned out, you had a sister. Not the little one everyone coddled and praised. You had Tina, our family's original cast-out. Tina, who could listen to story after story of rejection, not by some guy but by our own mother, and say, "I know exactly how you feel."

"Our neighborhood was actually too tame for Angie," Howie went on. "She liked the Tenderloin where the nightlife was edgier. Her heart was open to outcasts, which, at the time, were the transvestites and addicts. She could relate to them. That was her world. Angie was a lady of the night." His careful way of acknowledging how you made your money. "We'd rise with the kids sometime in the morning, and she wouldn't have gone to bed yet. While we got breakfast together, she'd describe the drug freak-outs and knife fights she witnessed the night before."

Howie told me how you often brought someone home with

you on those early mornings. "I want you to meet my boyfriend," you'd announce, though he and Tina soon learned that none of your relationships lasted more than a couple of weeks.

One was the biker named Big Bear, who I only knew by your tattoo.

"He'd walk over to the fridge and help himself to all our milk. I was a little afraid of him, so I wouldn't say anything. And anyway, you had to be cool about those things."

Howie put me in touch with his friend George, who had also lived with them at the time.

"Your sister was so blasé about everything," George noted when we spoke. "I couldn't imagine where she could have possibly come from. 'How old *were* you when you first hit the streets?' I used to ask her."

He told me that, if your boyfriends weren't strung out on amphetamines, it was on the painkillers you provided by going to the dentist, complaining of toothaches. At the mention of this, I shifted uncomfortably in my seat, recognizing in that detail a family trait I wasn't especially proud of. If there was a way to beat the system, Dad found it. Fudging numbers on forms, feigning interest in timeshares to qualify for discounted flights. He taught me that if lying about your age meant you paid less for your movie ticket, you lied about your age. If the cashier handed you too much change, you tucked the windfall in your pocket and considered it your lucky day.

"Once, your sister brought home an Elvis impersonator," George continued. "He had the gold suit, the slicked back hair, the whole deal. It would have been funny if it wasn't also so damn sad."

George told me that, by declining the pass you'd made at him when you first met, he earned your trust.

"The guy you met this morning?" you'd confide in him. "He's

174

the one, I know it. We're gonna get married."

"What happened to last week's 'the one?'" he'd tease. "I thought you were marrying him."

"That asshole? You don't even want to know what that M.F. did to me."

"You're right, I probably don't," George agreed, having witnessed enough of the explosions that ended your relationships.

Meanwhile, your access to the medicine for your epilepsy was erratic at best, and your seizures grew to grand mal proportions. They could be set off simply by startling you, so your housemates made a point of never coming up behind you or entering a room unannounced. Still, you sometimes fell down on the floor, your body wracked by its own electrical current.

Afterwards, as Tina hovered over you, you'd insist, "It's no big deal."

I considered, for the first time, how frightening it must have been for you to know you might lose consciousness at any moment. Crossing a busy street, standing on an overcrowded bus, entering a stranger's apartment. Once, you came to with your back pressed against a hot radiator. I'd seen the wide brown scar, heard you tell the story, but you had been marked by so much by then, I barely let myself give it any thought.

George went on to tell me about the morning you came home bruised and disheveled, your clothes torn, your stockings bunched in your hand.

"What happened?" Tina asked, flitting around you.

You brushed off her concern. "I had a hard night. Do me a favor and get me some coffee?"

"Are you hurt? Do you need to see a doctor?" Tina pressed while Howie and George sat at the table in stunned silence.

"No, really. I just want a cup of coffee."

"But what…"

"Some guy raped me, okay?" you finally blurted.

As George relayed this story, I recalled that long-ago evening in the Catskills when you whispered to me that you'd almost been raped. You were clearly terrified, but had to stop to define the word for me, your eight-year-old confidant who, of course, couldn't help you at all.

This time, as soon as you had your coffee poured and sugared, you seemed calm. "It's no big deal. I'm fine. Really."

A few weeks later, you lay on the couch in what was nearly a full body cast after the car accident that almost killed you.

"Can I get you anything?" everyone in the apartment took turns asking.

"I'm fine," you told them, as if this was just more of what you'd come to expect from life.

"Same story, different day," you used to say.

I soon discovered that the transients you befriended were known in the area as Seventh Street types. But to each other, you were a street family. And in your own way, you looked out for one another. I learned that, in addition to the Jack in the Box I remembered, you all hung out at a place called the Broil Burger. According to your good friend, Rose Marie Hunt, you'd get together and have group discussions. "What can I say? It was like a coffee klatch," she said.

I know that when Rose was new to the city, you let her stay with you, though I'm not sure if that was at Howie and Tina's place or if you had your own apartment then. When she was the one with a steady address, she let you receive your welfare checks there. Rose did what she could to get you out of prostitution. Early in your friendship, she convinced you to move with her to Florida where you both worked as hotel chambermaids. But you only lasted eight months before you were drawn back to San Francisco's streets.

Rose described your two-month dalliance with heroin, adding that your real love was speed, amphetamine and methamphetamine taken intravenously. She said you once injected codeine into your shoulder, but had an allergic reaction and wound up hospitalized.

On learning these details, I yearned to rewrite our first visit to San Francisco so that Mom stared directly into your haunted eyes and demanded you fly home with us. "You're going straight to rehab, young lady. And after that, you'll stay home and let me take care of you until you're responsible enough to take care of yourself." But in the version I'm stuck with, Mom sighed and shook her head, and we boarded the plane without you. I started tenth grade, and you went back to the Tenderloin District, looking for trouble in my favorite pair of broken-in jeans.

Not long after you returned to California, Rose followed, landing a job at the Broil Burger. One evening, she accidentally spilled coffee on a biker known as Hawaiian Jimmy. He grabbed her by the wrist.

"If you can't pour coffee properly, I'll do it myself," he said through gritted teeth.

A large, well-built man sitting at a nearby table came to Rose's defense.

"I mean it, Jimmy," Ray Boggs said, rising to his full height. "Leave the lady alone."

On another evening, you had a seizure in the Broil Burger, sputtering and kicking on the dirty floor. Ray, who was again eating there after work, cushioned your head, directed the crowd to stand back, and called 911.

According to Rose, the next time you ran into Ray at the Broil Burger, he said, "You need a place to stay where someone can care for you. Marry me?"

And from what you told me, you eyed him skeptically and answered, "Yeah, sure. Just get me a ring."

Chapter Twenty-Nine

A chivalrous man came to your aid in your moment of need and fell for you at a glance. It's the happy ending, the promise of a future, in all the Disney fairytale movies we watched together as kids.

Had you lived to meet my husband Dan, one of the first things he'd have asked would be for you to tell that story. He's always as eager to hear how couples met as he is to describe how our own love story began.

I had gone to a writing conference in Cape May, New Jersey, back when Ethan was eight, to study with a poet I admired named Stephen Dunn. Just before the workshop started, a tall blind man came into the room and was guided to the seat beside mine. I was struck right away by Dan's gentle, soft-spoken manner and the thoughtful feedback he offered the other writers at our table. When he brought out his own poem to be critiqued, I liked him even more. His piece had wit and heart. I couldn't help noticing we both mentioned ex-spouses in our poems.

After the workshop, we stayed in our seats a few extra minutes, talking. Then he slipped his hand into the crook of my arm, and we strolled together to the next event. I wondered if he noticed the lilt in my walk, and actually hoped that he did. I wanted him to know that, along with poetry, disability was something we shared.

When Dan phoned me a week later, we spoke for four hours. We discovered that we both had day jobs in libraries, confided in each other about our former marriages, read our favorite poems aloud, and discussed living with our very different disabilities.

Long before this, Dan had begun to write beautifully and candidly about his life as a blind man. Getting to know him and his work inspired me to take on disability as a subject, first in poems and then in a monthly column for an online journal called *Literary Mama*. It was there that I first described how motherhood had changed me, revealing through the physical challenges it brought into my life that my cerebral palsy wasn't just some cosmetic flaw I could occasionally feel bad about, but mostly ignore. Writing about how damaged and inadequate I felt was scary at first, like pulling my childhood brace out of the closet and putting it on display. But I'd actually tapped into something really relatable and wound up touching people. Also, though I didn't yet know it, by working on these personal essays—honing my skills, learning to write what had once seemed unspeakable—I was getting ready for this. Getting ready for you.

These days, Dan and I have a community of friends who are writers and artists with disabilities. We've built this rich, wonderful life together, but back on that long-ago night of our initial phone call, I couldn't have imagined any of it. What felt remarkable then was how easily we opened up to each other, and how familiar he seemed. It felt as though we'd picked up the dropped thread of an ongoing conversation. Oh, there you are, I found myself thinking. I know you.

I'm sure you felt a similar sense of recognition when you and Ray first talked about your lives. From what his brothers have told me, Ray was the rebel of the family, often in trouble, struggling in school. As the middle child, he could be measuring and jealous. Whatever they had—ice cream, money, attention—he tended to feel like he got the smallest share.

The first time I spoke to Ray's older brother Joseph, he nearly undid me by how much he sounded like Ray. Ray, Ray, Ray, my blood sang at the sound of that resonant voice. His manner slow and measured, yet warm. My eyes stung and I realized that, for the first time in three numb decades, I missed your guy. As Joseph described his brother's longing and envy, I pictured you and Ray curled together trading family stories—"You think you got a raw deal, listen to this"—and imagined you began to love the little girl you'd once been by recognizing parts of her in him.

It stunned me to discover that Ray even had half-siblings he and his brothers were barely aware of growing up. An older sister who was raised by their dad's family in Kentucky. Another sister who, in Joseph's words, had been *farmed out* to their mother's people. They also had a younger half-brother whose arrival was laden with rumors.

"Sounds like my family," I marveled, and told Joseph about the secrecy surrounding our own half-siblings, and how I'd only just had it confirmed that you and I shared a biological father.

"Angie and Ray definitely had a lot to connect over," he said.

"Damn straight," I blurted, and as soon as the words left my mouth, I heard how much I sounded like you.

I'd always sensed that, in Ray, you'd found someone who not only loved you, but *got* you. Yet, I hadn't really considered what a relief it must have been, after being on your own your whole life, to finally feel so understood. Knowing that you'd had that came with its own wash of relief. But, of course, it also felt bittersweet. You had the beginnings of what could have been a long, vibrant, surprising life together. For the first time ever, you had plenty to lose.

Days before my conversation with Joseph, I'd spoken to his younger brother, Terry, whose voice—its depth and cadence—reminded me of Steve, our own brother, who had only recently died. Rocking on a glider out on my terrace, I slipped off my shoes and closed my eyes as we talked.

"Ray was a great brother," Terry told me. "The only hard part was he'd disappear all the time. He'd go off on adventures, then call us from God knows where."

"Same with Angie!" I blurted.

I wondered if, like me, Terry was an incurable night owl, afraid that, if he let his guard down, the people he loved and counted on would leave him as he slept.

"Tell me more," I said.

Terry shared the story of how Ray got his panel truck, describing how Ray found himself in a traffic jam on the highway where there was a huge fire underway. He climbed out of his car and joined the crew working to put out the blaze. In appreciation, one of the guys there sold him the vintage truck for a dollar.

Terry also reminisced about dropping in on Ray at work during lunch breaks.

"Glass Tech was just three blocks from my house in Redwood City. I'd stay to watch *Perry Mason* with Ray on this little black-and-white TV he had in the office. He loved *Perry Mason*."

"That's a courtroom drama, right?" I had a vision of Ray watching the Henderson trial unfold on a black-and-white screen up in heaven, but I didn't share that with Terry. I wasn't ready to shift the conversation from Ray's life to his death. "What else do you remember?"

"The ladies loved Ray," Terry continued. "He went through a new girlfriend practically every day. But that changed with Angie. He was crazy about her. Sometimes, she'd come to my place to wait for him to finish up at work. When Ray walked in and saw her there, he just lit up. He'd hug and kiss her and steal a grope. She was good for him. Ray cleaned up his act for her."

"I always thought he was the good influence," I mused. "I

thought she got it together for him."

"Guess they were good for each other," he said.

Good for each other. That's how it always works when it works, right? If you're fortunate enough to find someone who fits you in that way, the person they see when they look at you is the best possible version of yourself, so you begin to not only see it too, but become it—for them, but also for you.

Other than the hours Ray spent at Glass Tech, I learned from your friend Rose Marie Hunt, the two of you were inseparable.

"Ray once told me he had three loves," Rose said. "One was his truck, one was his rifle, and one was Angie."

She also described how, when you moved into Ray's trailer in a South San Francisco RV Park, far from your favorite burger joints, you realized you had no idea how to cook. I love knowing that Rose came out to teach you basic kitchen skills, and that, a few months later, when you were pregnant with Ray-Ray, she stayed over to help you get to your medical appointments. Rose said that, in your last trimester, your hands and feet swelled like water balloons. Though you normally wore a seven and a half shoe like me, she took you shopping for size nines.

"It's your nutrition," the doctor admonished after you confessed to a diet of chips, candy, and as many as eight Pepsis a day. Yet, though you weren't eating well, you did manage to stay clean of drugs for this pregnancy and the next.

According to Rose, the trailer park didn't allow children, which is how you came to move to the apartment on Webster Street, walking distance from Jack in the Box where you spent your afternoons, Ray-Ray in tow, waiting for Ray to return from work.

Angie, I'm tempted to leave these pages unfinished here, as though doing so would keep you safely in a marriage where you each brought out the best in the other. With a friend who was like a big sister to you. And a baby who, I'm sure, like mine, had begun to teach you things about yourself you never knew.

But, of course, the story goes on.

Ray was promoted to foreman at Glass Tech, but money stayed tight, and he often had to ask for small advances on his pay. Apparently, that's where the Hendersons came in. You invited them to move in with you and Ray around Thanksgiving to help with the rent. Soon, Rose noticed a change in you. She described how the two of you used to meet every other week or so for lunch and a stroll through the park in Chinatown. But suddenly, you had no interest in getting together. When Rose called to press you about it, you were brusque and cold.

"It was like, 'Well, I've got things to do, okay?'" she explained. "It was like she didn't have time to be with me."

Rose said that, on January 5, she ran into you at a pharmacy. You both had prescriptions that would take time to fill, so you went to Jack in the Box together to wait. Ray-Ray's first birthday was coming up, and you discussed plans for a small party. Rose offered to bake a cake. While you talked, she marveled at your pregnant belly, but also noticed that you seemed terribly on edge. Ordinarily, you liked to sit in the front of the restaurant near the windows facing Market Street. But, that afternoon, you chose a booth near the back and kept glancing around, as if, Rose thought, you were afraid to be seen.

At some point, a man Rose didn't know came over to your table.

"I want to talk to you," he said to you, and you followed him to another booth.

Half an hour passed before you finally slid back into your seat across from Rose, who sensed you were even more upset.

She described how you wrung your hands like you were trying to squeeze the perspiration from them. Rose wanted to ask what had you so worried, but she recalled that strained phone call a month earlier.

"What's wrong?" Rose had asked then. "How can I help?"

"No one can help," you'd said.

What occurred to me when I first learned of this conversation was how frequently you must have thought that in your life. Though probably what you most often thought was, "No one will."

Meanwhile, I'll never know what you were so frightened of that afternoon in Jack in the Box, four days before my arrival in San Francisco, six days before your death. Was the man who had come to your table, and then left you so distraught, Philip Henderson? Rose didn't specify, and I can't ask now because she died before I had a chance to meet her. Every anecdote and quote from her here—about your medical history, your early days with Ray, your friendship with her—comes from the transcripts of Philip Henderson's murder trial.

Chapter Thirty

This last part of my search began soon after my conversations with Howie and George. One evening, spent from a long workday filled with dry meetings, I stretched beside Dan on our bed as he listened to music from the part of my childhood I got to share with you. He's ten years older than I am, so those hits from the sixties were the soundtrack of his teen years. As the Beatles sang "Hello, Goodbye," I lazily checked my email and browsed Facebook. On a whim, I typed *Ray and Angie Boggs* into a Google search box, expecting nothing. When an article from the San Francisco Bay Guardian came up, listing things to do and see in the city, I scrolled through it, baffled at first, and then appalled.

"Five stairways to the stars... The last five great movie theater deals...30 Bay Area Based Record Labels..." It went on and on. "13 murals by Rigo...Five clubs offering dance lessons..." Finally, "Scary San Francisco: six places where bad things happened."

The writing was jaunty. "Sure, this is a great town with beautiful architecture and breathtaking views, wonderful people, first-class restaurants, sourdough bread, blah, blah, blah. But let's not gloss over the truth: this place is also a magnet for sickos..."

753 Webster was number five on the list of crime scenes.

"Even many true-crime buffs don't know about the Crawl Space Killers. The year was 1982. The victims, an entire family... The Boggs clan were [sic] done in by their erstwhile friends, Wayne and Velma Henderson, who shot and strangled the family, stuffed their corpses into the crawl space under this four-unit apartment building, and took off with their money and pet parrot. Veteran homicide inspectors called to the scene were chilled."

Heart pounding, I leapt off the bed and began pacing, my lethargy melted by a clear, hot sense of purpose. Seeing the home where the three of you had been viciously killed made into a ghoulish tourist attraction confirmed for me that your story needed to be reclaimed by someone who loved you. No matter how flawed that love may have been.

Ethan was fourteen then and, most years, he, Dan, and I went out west for our vacations. Steve had always been our nexus during those visits, but now that he'd lost his decade-long battle with cancer, it was his kids and Tina's we flew there to see. Adults in their twenties and thirties, they lit me up with a familial love and recognition that still caught me off guard, having had so little contact with relatives growing up.

That August, in 2011, I traveled to the Bay Area alone and slept on a foldout futon in our niece Naomi's cozy apartment in Oakland. The summer before, she'd married the boy she had loved since she was twelve. Now, the three of us lingered in their plant-filled kitchen over breakfast each morning of my ten-day stay before Naomi dropped me at the BART station on her way to work. I'd exit the train at the Civic Center stop in San Francisco and spend the day trying to learn all I could about what happened to you, Ray, and little Ray-Ray.

Hour after hour, I sat hunched before a microfilm reader in the periodicals room of the public library on Larkin Street. It was there that I found an obituary for Ray, "...fond brother of JoAnn, Mary, Joseph, Terry, and Vincent."

This is hard to admit, but until that sad square of newsprint came up on the screen, it had never occurred to me to seek out Ray's family. Now, I posted a message to every JoAnn, Mary, Joseph,

Terry, and Vincent Boggs on Facebook. Responses poured in.

"Sorry, I am not that person."

"I did have a brother, but his name was David. Good luck in your search."

And finally, "Yes, this is Ray's brother, Terry. I have been thinking of Angie's family for so many years now, never knowing how to contact them or what to do. You can call me at --- --- ----."

One morning, I explored the city with our nephew Herman, Tina's oldest, whom I'd first met when, still in diapers, he came with his parents to our house in Far Rockaway in my eleventh summer. When he was twelve and I was a grad student at NYU, he flew to New York alone, and I took him to the coolest spots I could think of—Washington Square Park, Bob's Records, the comics shop on Saint Marks Place—only to discover that what he most wanted was a tour of the New York Stock Exchange. Now in his late thirties, he ran a popular inn in Mendocino and still called me "AuntOna" like it was one word, as though he understood how much it's meant to me since I'd first learned of that lovely piece of my identity back when he was four.

Herman and I wandered the wide dirty streets of the Western Addition. We checked if Jack in the Box was still standing. It wasn't. We showed photos of you and Ray to strangers to see if anyone recognized and remembered you. No one did.

Finally, we came to the small, cheerless green apartment house at 753 Webster Street.

"Does it look familiar at all?" Herman asked as we stood in the chill and fog of a typical San Francisco summer day.

I shook my head. "It's been nearly thirty years..."

The entrance was locked behind a tall black gate, preventing us from approaching the door and peeking inside. What the building resembled was my own gated-up, ancient grief. Did the key to unlocking that sorrow live in news articles on microfilm, or in the damp air of the city where you had lost your life? I didn't yet know.

By late February 1982, your soft-spoken landlord, Ilyas Absar, had come to believe that you and Ray had furtively left town. You'd stopped paying the rent and answering the phone, and hadn't responded to the notices, which he first mailed to you, then later taped to the door. For nearly two months, mail piled up outside your apartment.

When Ilyas called Glass Tech, he learned that Ray's supervisor hadn't seen him either. "Ray hasn't been coming to work. This isn't like him."

Ilyas understood that you had been struggling financially. That was why, when it came to his attention back in November that you'd brought in another couple, he chose not to say anything, though he could have charged more for the extra people. He knew Ray to be a good man who was trying hard to take care of his growing family. The boarders were clearly there to help with the bills.

The last time they'd spoken, Ilyas had been taken aback by how meek Ray sounded, like a mouse caught in a trap. "Please sir," Ray had said. "I need more time." The pleading in his voice really got to Ilyas. No man should be in this position, he thought.

Finally, Ilyas reluctantly entered Apartment C with a friend to begin clearing it out. It surprised them to find one of the two rooms completely emptied while the other was full of stuff, all in disarray.

As the two men began boxing your things, Ilyas was struck by the fact that there was no loose change in the place. In his experience, there were always a couple of dimes or a quarter tucked beneath the sofa cushions or left in a neglected corner. But here, it seemed, someone had gone through and collected everything of value down to a cent.

Ilyas put the furniture out on the street. He had intended to donate the rest of your deserted belongings to the Salvation Army, but the apartment turned out to be infested with fleas. On February 28, he arranged for someone to meet him who could haul the boxes to the dump. After they'd loaded everything from the apartment into the truck, Ilyas asked the driver to take some items from the crawlspace, where he'd noticed a lot of junk piling up. There was a big package down there that was so heavy the men couldn't lift it. They managed to move the bundle about ninety degrees and, when they did, a noxious stench rose up. The driver refused to take it with him.

"No, that smells too bad," he said. "I'm not handling that."

After the driver left, Ilyas wondered what the foul-smelling bundle contained. He'd assumed it was old clothes, but then why would it be so heavy? When he peeled back the cloth, he saw a man's arm.

"It was the worst moment of my life," Ilyas told me when we spoke three decades later. "I couldn't even look at food, especially meat, for a very long time."

"The badly decomposed body of a man bound at his wrists and ankles was discovered by a hotel manager cleaning his backyard yesterday," read a tiny article in the San Francisco Examiner under the headline, "Body Found Rolled Up in Rug."

The paper had some of the details wrong, but, Angie, they were right about how Ray had been tied. When I'd read this at the library, days before my conversation with Ilyas, I assumed Ray was bound after his death to make his body easier to move. But Ilyas corrected me. According to the police, Ray had been shot execution style, hog-tied and forced to lie helplessly, his own rifle pressed against his head. The bullet, they'd discover during his autopsy, had drastically mushroomed upon hitting his skull. This happens when someone has taken the time to carve crosscuts into the metal to shorten the projectile and increase its power upon impact, something Philip Henderson would later admit to knowing how to do.

"It's unbelievable what people do to each other," Ilyas mused as we were saying goodbye.

That night, as I lay in my borrowed bed, I couldn't stop thinking about Ray. I remembered his strength and also how calm and unflappable he'd always seemed. Even after you were carted off with Dad to spend the night in jail, with Ray-Ray due any minute, Ray appeared to take it in stride. A year later, when I spoke to him for the last time, the worry I heard in his voice was accompanied by firm resolve. He was on a mission to find you, his mind clicking through a mental Rolodex for who to call and what next steps to take to set the world right again. The idea that, minutes later, the Hendersons literally brought him to his knees and slaughtered him like an animal left me shaking and barely able to breathe.

For three weeks, after Ray's body was discovered, no one knew what had happened to you and the baby, or where you might have gone. Then, on March 19, your neighbor from apartment A, Ronald Ashley, was out in the yard with his children when he noticed a terrible odor emanating from the crawlspace. He ushered his kids into the house and flagged down a passing patrol car.

"I remembered what happened last month," Ronald explained to reporters, "and I told my kids, 'Let's get out of here because I'm afraid of this place.'"

A swarm of flies led police ten feet further back from where Ray's body had lain to two more bundles hidden behind a discarded headboard. Ronald recognized the wrappings as bedding from your apartment.

"The two bodies found yesterday, described by the coroner only as a pregnant white woman in her twenties and an infant of indeterminate sex, have not been positively identified," the Examiner reported on March 20, 1982. "The general description, however, fits Boggs' missing wife and son."

The article includes a photograph of the crawlspace with what appears to be a parent and child burrowed side by side in sleeping bags. Also visible are discarded two-by-fours, a box containing toys or Christmas decorations, a lone work boot, and a grinning plastic jack-o-lantern.

As I stared at the grainy image, I remembered trick-or-treating with you. I also remembered how I'd glance across our shared bedroom, in the early morning, at your sleeping form. "Wake up, Andra," I whispered there in the library. As though that incantation could drop us both back beneath our matching quilts, surrounded by yellow walls and lace curtains. As though the house that contained that room had been as safe a place for you as it had been for me.

"Investigators apparently missed the other two bodies when Boggs was taken away. [They] were also wrapped in blankets and tucked around the corner of a building support, sharing the crawlspace with the bodies of poisoned rats as well as those of several domestic cats who had died after eating the rats..."

So that's what happened to the kittens, I thought as I saved the article, "S.F. Police Have Not a Clue About Three Neatly Wrapped Bodies," on my thumb drive. *My babies*, you'd called them on the last afternoon of your life, lifting one up to hold the warmth of its small, soft body against your own.

The following evening, when I'd talked to Ray, he told me that, according to Philip and Velma, you'd gotten a phone call that afternoon and gone out. Now, scrolling through another article,

I learned that the Hendersons had repeated this lie the first time they spoke to the police. But as soon as your decomposing body was unwrapped from its shroud of blankets and sheets, it became clear that you'd never left home on the final day of your life. You had on a nightie, panties, and one slipper.

A nightie. Slippers. Closing my eyes, I could hear you padding around your kitchen on what must have felt at first like an ordinary morning. I could picture you warming a bottle for Ray-Ray in a pan of water at the stove, your thick hair still an unbrushed tangle, the day still stretched before you like a promising road.

When the bodies arrived at the coroner's office, a yellow towel from that kitchen was still around your neck. How many times, I found myself wondering, had you mindlessly dried your hands on it or used it to wipe up a spill? Maybe you'd dipped a terry cloth corner under the faucet, mere days before it became a murder weapon, to carefully pat a crusted bit of baby food off Ray-Ray's chin.

As for your sweet boy, due to the extent to which his body had decomposed, and the fact that an adult can so easily kill such a small child, his cause of death couldn't be proved. According to the autopsy report, Ray-Ray—even without a face it was clearly him, a child of approximately one year with six toes on one of his little feet—had most likely been smothered.

Your other baby, referred to as Jane Doe and described by the coroner as a little leatherette statue at the time of your autopsy, had been a healthy, viable fetus who died because you did, cutting off her supply of oxygen and food.

Did you catch that, Angie? She would have been a girl—your daughter, my niece—just as you, Ray, and I had hoped.

Chapter Thirty-One

As I sat in my carrel at the library, it continually surprised me that this public record of what had happened to you existed. On some level, I knew the feeling didn't make sense. Of course the story was newsworthy. Of course these details could be found. But over those many years, I had buried the fact of your brutal deaths so deeply inside myself, it was almost as though the tragedy existed only in my imagination.

Now, here was proof. It had been real. Yet, even with this evidence before me, a disconnect remained. As I spun from article to article, the murders unfolding in much harsher and more graphic detail than what I'd learned from the inspectors back when I was nineteen, I didn't cry. I felt choked up at times, but I still couldn't truly mourn my kind and loving brother-in-law, my funny-faced nephew, or my big sister whose voice grew rich with earnestness when you explained your side of an argument and with pride when you introduced me to your friends. I might have been a crazed woman, curled and sobbing on the library floor. Instead, I calmly scanned my articles, thanked the librarian when she handed me my printouts, strolled back to the rows of metal cabinets to select another reel. What did that say about the kind of person I was? The kind of sister? Ashamed and unable to answer, I kept on.

Inspector Napoleon Hendrix first came upon the name Henderson when he contacted the telephone company and asked to see the bill for the phone in your apartment. The paperwork had it listed under "Phil W. Henderson." Hendrix assumed this to be an alias of Ray's, but when he called a Florida number listed on the bill, it was answered by Philip Henderson, who was staying with his mother there.

Inspector Hendrix asked him if he knew Ray. Philip hesitated before stating that yes, he and his wife had stayed with the two of you in San Francisco for a few weeks to help you with the rent. The inspector then asked whether you and Ray had a baby. Philip answered, "I think so," then paused and said, "I'm not sure."

Napoleon Hendrix, a father of three children, all quite conspicuous, took note.

Philip told the inspector that when he and Velma left San Francisco, they hitchhiked all the way east, though they had actually driven to Nevada in Ray's panel truck. When asked for the exact date they departed California, Philip gave January 11, 1982.

"Did that date have any special significance to you?" Bill Fazio, attorney for the People, would later ask Inspector Hendrix at Philip's trial.

"It did."

"What was that?"

"Last phone call emanating from Mr. Boggs' residence was on the 11th. I knew that Ray Boggs worked on the 11th. Never returned to work on the 12th. I knew that he had received a check advance on his salary on the 11th and the check was never cashed."

The coroner corroborated the date.

"San Francisco coroner Boyd Stephens says the life cycle of the common fly helped him determine how long a Western Addition couple and their infant had been dead after their badly decomposed bodies were discovered beneath the family's house," reads a December 1, 1982 article in the Examiner. "He said the maturity of the flies, how many generations of them were present, and the growth of new larvae and maggots could fairly well date the time of death...—which he pegged at January 11—of all three victims."

As I read about the maggots eating away at the bodies, there was no pretending this was someone else's tragedy. The article included a photograph of you and Ray holding Ray-Ray between you on your couch. Dad took that picture. I knew because I had the others in the set. You and Ray looking young, tough, and beautiful in the same clothes on that same couch. You and Dad propping Ray-Ray up to standing, the baby's tiny fingers touching Dad's cheek.

Swallowing past the lump in my throat, I opened another microfilm drawer and found the reel for the January 9-15, 1982 TV Guide. An Errol Flynn movie, *The Sea Hawk*, had aired on Sunday, January 10 at 8pm. This shook me as much as anything else I'd come across. This seemingly innocuous listing that matched my timeworn memory and placed me there in that room with Kay, Greg, and the couple who would, in a matter of hours, murder you, Ray, and baby Ray-Ray, then roll your bodies in bedding and throw them away.

Inspector Hendrix and his partner, Earl Sanders, opened a Triple A roadmap and began tracing the course the Hendersons had likely taken east, focusing on Highway 80 because of a storm that would have precluded other routes. Hendrix then called the police departments in each city along the way. Sacramento, Auburn, Tahoe. An officer in Reno informed him that, on January 12, a person by the name of Philip Wayne Henderson had used his I.D. to pawn a diamond ring.

The ring that Ray had given you for Christmas, yellow gold with a diamond chip at its center, was one of only two of a kind. The jeweler who sold it to Ray loaned the duplicate to the inspectors earlier in their investigation, and they'd photographed it from all angles. Taking those pictures with them, Inspectors Hendrix and Sanders headed to Reno. On the way, they received a call on their radio stating that Ray's truck had been located in the city of Carlin, Nevada, three hundred miles east of Reno. The Inspectors learned that the truck had broken down on January 13 when, upon hearing that it could take as long as two weeks to fix, a man identifying himself as Wayne Henderson threw a fit, then sold it to the owner of the garage, promising to mail the title once he returned home to Florida. Meanwhile, the truck sat in a lot, still displaying the license plates linking it to Ray.

Among the items found inside the truck was a letter addressed to Philip Henderson, "Free World Party Chairman." Inspector Hendrix was familiar with the Free World Party. It was a White supremacist group, a fact that Philip would later unsuccessfully attempt to suppress during his trial. That S.O.B. assumed they'd get away with it because they're White, I thought when I discovered that detail, and wondered if that vile confidence wavered when he met the two remarkable Black men who cracked the case.

After purchasing what was undeniably your ring at the Palace Jewelry and Loan Company in Reno, Hendrix and Sanders went to Carlin, where they learned that, after the truck broke down, the Hendersons had given the owner of a motel a green parrot in exchange for seventy-five dollars and a three-night stay.

"They claimed they left San Francisco after losing their home in a mudslide," the motel owner said.

The Hendersons then took a bus from Nevada to Salt Lake City, Utah, where they hitched a ride with a man named Mark Koci, to whom they admitted being "on the run." Koci drove them to Wyoming, where Philip tried to steal his car. When Koci caught him, Philip reportedly encouraged Velma to shoot the guy. The details are muddy in the brief article that mentions this, but it seems the police were called, and Philip was taken into custody. Soon, though, he was released, and Ray's rifle was returned to him. Later, Koci gave Inspectors Hendrix and Sanders a box of twenty-two caliber long bullets Philip had left in his car, several of which had been crosscut.

On April 29, 1982, just six weeks after your and little Ray-Ray's bodies were found, Philip and Velma were arrested in Florida and driven separately to the United States Marshal's office. While Philip refused to speak to the inspectors without a lawyer present, Velma waived her Miranda rights and agreed to an interview, which was recorded. She stated that she and her husband left your place on a Monday in January, taking very few of their belongings with them. They went to Berkeley by bus and from there were driven by acquaintances to Salt Lake City, Utah. Velma denied stopping in Reno, Carlin, or any other cities on the way. She had noticed that Philip brought along a rifle, but claimed she didn't know where it came from. Unaware that the inspectors had recovered these items in Nevada, she answered yes when asked if Ray had a green parrot he'd received as a gift from you and mentioned that you never took off the diamond ring you'd gotten for Christmas from him.

"Fine Sleuthing Solves S.F. Murders of Three," a headline in the April 30 issue of the Examiner reads.

"San Francisco homicide inspectors Napoleon Hendrix and Earl Sanders served the arrest warrants in Tampa last night, culminating an exhaustive investigation that covered at least four states and hundreds of leads..."

The day the article came out, Inspectors Hendrix and Sanders were still at work. Before leaving Florida, they visited Philip's mother to see if he and Velma had left anything relevant to the investigation in her home. When asked if her son was in possession of a gun, Philip's mother excused herself to make a call. Less than five minutes later, her neighbor knocked on the door. He had with him the bolt-action .22-caliber rifle he'd recently purchased from Philip. The serial number matched the rifle that had belonged to Ray and had hung above us while you showed me the box of kittens and while I sat with your murderers watching Errol Flynn swashbuckle across the screen on your little black-and-white TV.

Packing up for the night, I wondered anew about my own ability to look at such bleak, devastating details about people I had loved, and feel only a vague and muffled sadness.

"How'd it go today, Auntie?" Naomi asked an hour later when we met up in front of a Thai restaurant in Oakland, where her sister and two of her brothers were joining us for dinner.

"It's going," I answered, feeling as though my heart, like your bodies, had been tightly wrapped and tossed among years of neglected debris.

Chapter Thirty-Two

While I was in San Francisco, I met with a prosecutor from the DA's office, who helped me acquire part of Philip Henderson's trial transcripts. They arrived after I returned home, digitized and saved onto compact discs. I read them on a tablet, slogging through details about jury selection, testimony by gun experts, and graphic autopsy reports for the moments when your friends took the stand. These were people central to your life in a way I hadn't been since I was a very little girl, and the transcripts—in their present-tense immediacy—placed me there with them in the room.

As I've said, I felt especially drawn to Rose, who had been so good to you during your pregnancy with Ray-Ray, so nurturing and maternal, you named her his godmother.

"As far as you know," Michael Burt, Philip's defense attorney, asked her, "was Angie Gritz married to Raymond Boggs at any point in time before they died?"

"No she was not," Rose surprised me by saying. "...When she found out her parents and sister were coming into town from New York, she bought an old silver wedding set that I had."

My reaction as I read this was knotted and contradictory. "There's me!" I said aloud, like someone spotting herself in the crowd scene of a movie. At the same time, I felt stung that you had lumped me with our parents, lying to all of us.

I read the sentence again and was caught by the possibility that the ring set Rose mentioned might be the one Mom had snatched from you the week after Steve's wedding, when I was sixteen. That visit had pre-dated Ray, I felt sure. The set a gift from an earlier boyfriend. When I went to look, it turned out I was right. Those lovely rings were, as I'd remembered, gold. Holding them, I felt once again what a complicated inheritance they were. The only objects I have in the world that once belonged to you placed me squarely in our angry mother's camp.

Her camp. There should never have been camps in our family, but clearly there were, and yours, ultimately, had only one person in it. That, of course, was why you left, and also why you'd stopped letting me in on your secrets. On the long list of things I'll never know is whether, had you lived, you would have eventually opened up to me again. Not just about the intricacies of your relationship with Ray, but all of it. The sexual abuse, the reformatories, the fact that Dad was your biological father but hadn't wanted you to know. Could the closeness we shared in our youngest years have been rekindled? Would you have come to trust me again? Would I, if I still had you, have eventually grown brave enough to want to hear about your life?

I had no way to answer any of those questions, but I did have the transcripts. So, while Rose went on to describe how much Ray's Christmas gift of a diamond ring meant to you and revealed the plans you had with him to drive to Reno in a borrowed Cadillac convertible and marry for real, I took it in as though I was back in your confidence. "I wouldn't have told," I whispered.

But, of course, Philip's lawyer didn't summon your friends to court to reminisce. He brought them in to prove something about your way of life.

To supplement Ray's income, Rose admitted, you ran pot for someone in your building. "On the phone, or sometimes when we just passed at Jack in the Box, she'd mention if I knew anybody that wanted some quality stuff, she could get it for me."

Over the many months of my quest, I'd sought your friend Greg. Yet, while I learned his last name, Walker, from the back of an old photo the DA's office had on file, it proved too common to do me any good. Here, too, in the transcripts, he couldn't be found. Never called to testify. Not mentioned by name. One neighbor, however, was questioned by the defense about a tall Black man who was occasionally seen visiting you while Ray was at work. The implication, though never stated, was that you might have had affairs.

"The import of the evidence concerning lifestyle," Michael Burt asserted, "[is] not to cast aspersions on the people who were killed here. It's not to create prejudice in your mind. Its import [is] to understand we are not dealing with Ozzie and Harriet here."

Another friend of yours and Ray's, Ana Caquias, had told police during the initial investigation that she'd been asked, on occasion, to take the baby into another room of your apartment during drug transactions, and that Ray was in trouble because you had set up "bad deals."

What did that mean? I wondered as I read Michael Burt's rehashing of these statements. Had you trusted the wrong client? The wrong dealer? Had you deliberately tried to cheat someone? Flushing, I thought of our family's tendency to play the system and seek workarounds. Would you have tried such tricks when those in charge of the "system" were dangerous traffickers and thieves? I also thought back to that last night when you and Ray left the rest of us watching *The Sea Hawk* while you ran some undisclosed errand. Was the task drug related? Did it involve money the Hendersons had counted on as theirs?

Regardless, now, in court, Ana retracted her entire statement about the drugs.

"It was all a story. I just did a quarter gram the night before, and started drinking that morning...Have you ever been up for ten days and then give [sic] a statement? Your mind is not all there. Your body is, but your mind isn't...Your mouth talks, but you don't."

By the time I finished reading Ana's contradictory testimony, I felt wrung out. There was no way to decipher what was true, or how any of it fit in with the murders. Only one thing was clear. Despite his claim, Philip's lawyer had meant to cast aspersions. He brought in these witnesses to imply that you and Ray had died because of how you lived. It was a perspective I recognized painfully. "A social worker told us years ago that, with the way Andra lived her life, she wouldn't make it to thirty," Mom had said just days after your body was discovered. A decade later, when a good friend of mine joined the legions of vibrant young men to succumb to AIDS, I came to believe that you, Ray, and your children would have eventually died of the disease, *given the way you lived*.

"What bias does a witness have in coming into court?" Burt went on to ask. "If a defendant brings his mother in, and Mom takes the stand and says, 'He was home with me at the time this crime was committed,' the first thing the prosecutor does is stand up and say, 'You love your son, don't you?' Yes, it shows bias. Moms are going to come in and help out their kid. You don't have that situation in this case. You have the godmother of the child who was killed coming into court and telling you that Angie Boggs was apparently dealing some drugs out of her house."

Reading this, I felt hot with shame to be the only one of that absentee mother's children to have had her protection. Still, no matter how astute Michael Burt was about our family dynamics, it didn't slip past me that, through his analogy, he'd placed you in the position of defendant, essentially putting you on trial for your son's murder and, by extension, Ray's and your own. Ever since I could remember, you were always, in some way, the defendant. Always accused, always assumed to be wrong. "How is this my fault?" I could still hear you asking Mom in a shaky, disbelieving voice. That this could continue to happen to you posthumously stunned me to the point that I had to stop reading and leave the house. I found myself envying our little dog as she leapt with pure joy at the sight of me reaching for her leash.

It was a crisp fall day and, as I walked beneath trees blazing with color, I had the clear and simple realization that, whatever else was happening in those last weeks of your life, in the end, all you did was trust the wrong two people. You were in your twenties, the decade of risk. When I was that age, I brought strangers I met in Washington Square Park into my home and, a couple of times, into my bed. Maybe I was emulating you. Maybe, spinning with guilt and untapped grief, I was chasing your fate. But somehow, despite my questionable judgment, nothing bad happened to me. Your death, contrary to what Mom said, and what Michael Burt told the court, wasn't some foregone conclusion based on how you lived. It was the result of one understandable if disastrous choice.

And if you hadn't chosen to trust the Hendersons? What then?

Too spent to attempt to daydream a life for you through to the present, I placed you in the borrowed Cadillac convertible Rose described. Top down, your long hair streaming, Ray-Ray safely tucked in a car seat in back, Baby Jane Doe safely tucked in your womb. Rather than have you head toward your Reno wedding, I pictured you soaring home afterward, the pink expanse of the desert giving over to hills covered in pines. I saw Ray sitting perfectly upright at the wheel, proud to be your husband, and imagined that you, in turn, felt an unfamiliar sense of calm. As you neared the industrial patch that edges the city, Ray-Ray burbled and kicked his chubby legs, and Ray said something to you that made you smile. The Bay Bridge unfurled, and the bay appeared, vast and gleaming around you. You continued on.

Chapter Thirty-Three

I mentioned earlier that Dad had wanted to become a lawyer. With his plans thwarted, he briefly hoped I might choose that path. I couldn't have done it, I believed, given the dreamy, distractible way my mind works. But while reading the transcripts, it came to me that, when Philip's attorney questioned Rose about the pot you'd offered her and then brought in your drug-addled friend Ana, he was actually doing work I understood well. Drawing out just the details he needed, Michael Burt was shaping a story. One where you and Ray were big-time dealers, and the murderer wasn't his client, but someone long enmeshed in San Francisco's shady underworld of drugs. This strategy, I came to learn, is known as the alternative explanation defense, the third-party culpability defense, and even TODDI: the other dude did it defense.

"The other dude did it" was the assumption the Hendersons had counted on from the very beginning, possibly even before they'd actually taken your lives. They wanted everyone to believe that you and Ray owed money to the Hell's Angels and another violent biker gang, The Sons of Hawaii. Philip claimed that members of both gangs had threatened the two of you in his presence. He was particularly interested in pinning it on Hawaiian Jimmy, the man who had grabbed Rose's wrist when she'd spilled coffee on him at the Broil Burger the night she first met Ray. To this end, Philip cited a note he himself left next to a set of keys in your apartment. The note, which Ilyas Absar threw away when he came to clean, supposedly said something along the lines of "Sorry to skip out on you like this. This thing between Angie and Jimmy has us worried. We will send for our stuff later." He quoted his note as evidence in his own defense, despite how "We will send for our stuff later" must have sounded to the jury, given that he'd already confessed to stealing all of your belongings before leaving town. According to Philip, Hawaiian Jimmy, furious over an unpaid debt, had once beaten Ray on the head with a metal cane. I could imagine you and Ray laughing at this prospect; when Edward Ramos, A.K.A. Hawaiian Jimmy, was called to the stand, he proved to be a short, overweight asthmatic who needed that cane to walk. He testified that Ray did owe him money, but it was for work he'd done on the panel truck. Ray was paying it off until the time of his death—there were cancelled checks to prove this—fifty dollars at a time.

As for the Hell's Angels, nothing could be found linking them to you and Ray.

"Philip claimed some bikers did it, which was just ridiculous," Bill Fazio, the attorney who'd prosecuted the case, said when we met in his office after one of my long afternoons culling articles at the San Francisco Public Library. "Why would bikers do it? If they did it to make a statement, they wouldn't have hidden the bodies. It was just so crazy. The jurors didn't buy it at all."

The evidence against the Hendersons was simply too over-whelming. Most damning among all the items they'd taken from you and sold was Ray's rifle. A forensic expert testified that the bullet retrieved from Ray's head was the exact type that went with that rifle, identical to the bullets Philip left behind in Mark Koci's car and crosscut like most of those had been.

The alternative explanation defense was thrown out through a statute known as the Mendez-Arline Exclusionary Rule. As with other legal terms I came across as I studied the transcripts, I carefully copied this down.

The defense's only other hope was to cast doubt on the date of your death, a crucial detail since, by January 12, the Hendersons were out of the state. While both sides agreed that Ray had been missing since January 11, Burt asked why, if you were killed the same day, hadn't the police noticed your body when they recovered his. He maintained that they didn't find it because it wasn't yet there.

In response, Bill Fazio reminded the jury that your and Ray-Ray's corpses were already badly decayed when they were found on March 19, and went on to ask, "So, where was she during this period of time? If she is dead somewhere else, does somebody take her body and the body of the child in the disgusting, gross, decomposed condition that they were in, go into the Boggses' residence, through this door that is usually locked, the garbage door, go in there after the police discover the body of Ray, climb over the boxes, and deposit them there? No, I don't think so."

The question of when you were killed lay most heavily on your landlord. In a taped statement Ilyas had given just a few months after the murders, he told the inspectors he'd last spoken to you on the Wednesday of either January 13 or 20, when you'd called asking for his help in settling an argument with your neighbor Carol regarding a Big Wheel in the hallway. But then he began to doubt himself. Maybe you'd called on a Monday, and it was on a Wednesday that he finally made it over to Webster Street to try to resolve the issue. That day, no one answered at Apartment C.

When Ilyas expressed his uncertainty at the preliminary hearing some months later, the defense pressed him hard. Finally, exhausted and, he would tell me on the phone decades later, petrified by the threatening way Philip glared at him from across the room, that mild-mannered man lost patience with the defense.

"Just because my testimony was being recorded at the time

does not mean that that is just a hundred percent true. And at this time, I am supposed to give you a hundred percent truth as I know it, and I couldn't swear to either the 13th or the 20th as the date."

In the three-plus years leading up to Philip's trial, Ilyas worked to pinpoint the exact date he last spoke to you. He knew for certain that he'd had dinner later that night with two couples, the Markwards and the Mosses. Mrs. Moss, as it happened, maintained a datebook in 1982. Her dinner with Ilyas and the Markwards proved to be on January 11. Still, the defense continued to insist that Ilyas's first recollection of the date was correct. "He was questioned too often. He grew confused."

Had this been some fictional drama you and I were watching on TV, like Ray's beloved *Perry Mason*, you'd have appreciated Bill's biting response to this argument.

"January 11th, the defendant tells us, they cleaned the Boggses out. He took the van, the parrot, he took the gun. He took everything that they owned. 'Everything,' he said by his own admission. Now think about it. Did Angie Boggs come home sometime on the 12th or 13th, walk into her apartment, husband is gone because nobody's ever seen him again, the van is gone, the bird is gone...And did she call up her landlord on January 13th and say, 'Hi Mr. Absar. This is Angie. Can you come over to the house and straighten out a dispute between my neighbor and me over the tricycle in the hallway?'...Wouldn't she have called the police?... Wouldn't you do something?"

To further prove your date of death, the prosecution called a clerk from the records department of Children's Hospital, who testified that you missed your prenatal appointment on January 12, basing this on your file, which showed that you hadn't had your vitals taken and no notes were made. Then, the coroner was questioned over how certain he was that the fetus you were carrying had stopped growing at thirty weeks. This fact was essential to the case for two reasons. Not only would your unborn baby's age help confirm when you'd been killed, it would decide whether the Hendersons could be convicted of a fourth murder. At thirty weeks, the baby may have survived outside your womb. Her death, therefore, would constitute a homicide.

Ultimately, because you had been given a sonogram on December 30 that could be compared to x-rays taken of the baby after your autopsy, it was impossible for the defense to dispute that your would-be daughter had stopped growing at thirty weeks. Together with Rose's testimony, it also told me something I wouldn't have otherwise known. Despite your financial troubles and whatever entanglements you got caught up in through the wiliness you'd first learned, as had I, in the house we grew up in, you'd been a good mother. You stayed clean. You made and kept your medical appointments. Contrary to the picture Michael Burt and Mom tried to paint, and the perceptions I had carried all those years, you'd become someone who could, in fact, be counted on.

"I don't know how you do it," Dan commented when I told him over dinner what I'd read and figured out that day. It wasn't the first time he'd said it, and he wasn't the only one to remark on the grim and heartbreaking exploration that now obsessed me. Of course, I also felt boggled by my capacity for gathering such wrenching facts with the dispassion of a reporter, or of the diligent student you used to tease me for being. What kind of sister does that make me? I asked myself, just as I had in the San Francisco library. But, Angie, this time the question landed differently. Though I could only barely touch the bruised and tender edges of my grief, these months of probing felt deeply important. Thirty years after the fact, I had finally come to bear witness. "About time, Miss Educated," I could almost hear you say.

Chapter Thirty-Four

The jury convicted Philip Henderson of two counts of first-degree murder for you and Ray, voluntary manslaughter for Ray-Ray, and second-degree murder for the fetus. Velma's trial, which used the same evidence and witnesses, ultimately ended in a matching verdict. In the summer of 1986, as I watched, alone on a hard bench in the back of the courtroom, they were each given four consecutive life sentences without the possibility of parole.

"Did anyone ever learn their motive?" I'd asked Bill Fazio the evening he and I had sat together in an empty conference room, talking quietly as the patch of sky visible through the high windows grew dark. Younger than I expected, Bill reminded me of the actor Michael Keaton with his black curls and warm sad eyes.

"We'll never know for sure," he said. "What I think happened is there was an argument with Angie. Maybe over the baby. Maybe over money. Maybe she caught them stealing. So they got into a fight, and it escalated, and they wound up killing Angie and then they killed the baby. Or the other way around."

After pausing to reflect back through the years, he added that Inspectors Hendrix and Sanders came to believe that it started with Ray-Ray. That his crying woke Philip up that final morning, and he flew into a rage.

It's plausible. I'd soon read in the transcripts that, days before the murders, Philip had ranted and cursed at the five-year-old son of your neighbors Ronald and Carol over where the child had left his Big Wheel. That same small issue you had attempted to resolve in the last few hours of your life.

But when I shared this theory with my friend Kay, she dismissed it. "That baby barely made a peep the whole day we were with him. Plus, if the guy was so sensitive to noise, why would they take the squawking parrot with them?" Kay felt certain the murders were planned, and that, assuming it was Velma who had called Mom, warning her to keep me away from you and Ray, she already knew what she and Philip were going to do.

Once Kay said that, I saw a link between Philip's tie to a White supremacist group and that mysterious call. Velma—it had to be her—made a point of telling Mom that I was on a date with a Black man. At the time, I'd brushed the whole episode off, thinking of it as odd but basically meaningless. But maybe Velma had meant to drop a crumb that could later lead away from her and Philip in an investigation. You were in some kind of trouble, she'd insisted. But if, as Kay suggested, that trouble was something still in the works, Velma might have brought up Greg to imply that whatever danger lay ahead couldn't possibly come from a nice White couple like her and her husband. Whiteness as preemptive alibi. Mom and I as pawns in their plot.

And if your and Ray's murders were premeditated, little Ray-Ray's must have been as well.

"How do you explain the death of an eleven-month-old?" Bill had asked in his closing argument. "... Is a child going to testify? No, of course not. Is a child going to point the finger against someone? Of course not...I could only conclude that there is certain truth to that book title, *Murder and Madness*. Maybe those terms are interchangeable...Maybe it takes a lunatic to kill an eleven-month-old child. And if that's the only explanation I have for you, that's because I can think of no other."

During my meeting with Bill, he'd brought out a large, matted drawing and placed it on the table before me. "Philip was some kind of tattoo artist," he explained. "This was left among the evidence. I kept it because I found it fascinating."

"Philip did this?" I stared at a skillfully rendered image of a skull with a snake slithering up through the space where its missing jaw would be and twisting out through one of its eyeholes. Philip had dated the piece '82, which meant he'd completed it within ten days before the murders. In stiff stylized letters, he'd written the word *Enforcer*, the legs of his R's crossed like crucifixes fallen to the ground.

Chilled, I pulled out the envelope of pictures our nephew Herman and I had shown to strangers on Market Street and handed it to Bill, as though a glimpse of you, Ray, and grinning little Ray-Ray could work as antidotes to Philip's sinister drawing.

Bill carefully studied each photo, then said, "Thank you" so quietly I barely heard.

You had mattered to him, I realized in that moment, even though you'd never met. You and Ray and your children. For so long, I'd let myself believe that how I lost you was something personal and private, mine to acknowledge or not. But now, finally, I understood just how many people were affected by the crime. Ilyas, who opened a bundle of what he assumed was dirty clothes and found a corpse. The coroner, who had to cut your unborn daughter out of your womb. All those who, along with Bill, made solving the case their life's work for a time: Napoleon Hendrix, Earl Sanders, even the defense team, and the jurors, who stepped out of their own lives for months to listen to the disturbing details.

For the first time in decades, I considered how Kay must have felt living by herself in a hotel room in that suddenly terrifying city. I also thought of Ray's father, who had called our house in tears, and his mother, who signed the paperwork and made the funeral arrangements for her son, daughter-in-law, and grandchildren. And, finally, there were Ray's brothers, two men whose losses mirrored my own. Acknowledging all this felt dangerous at first, and then freeing. I didn't have to carry it alone.

One evening, in the weeks when I was immersed in the trial transcripts, I found myself admitting on the phone to Joseph Boggs that, after poring over those harrowing pages, my sleep was no more troubled than usual. I told him I'd always found it difficult to wind down at a decent hour, an issue I attributed to how you'd sneak out of our shared room while I slept during my youngest, most formative years. This was a piece of our history I talked about easily. But now I also confided in this man, who had referred to himself in a recent email as my brother-in-law once removed, a facet of my dreadful sleep habits I'd never told anyone.

"It's hard for me to get out of bed most mornings and, as I lie there, what I'm doing is berating myself. That's how I start my day, every day. By basically listing all my faults and mistakes." My voice cracked and I paused, surprised by what I was about to say. "I think it's because I feel guilty for getting to wake up at all."

"Survivor syndrome," Joseph, a war veteran and retired psychologist, responded in his deep, achingly familiar voice. "It's an aspect of PTSD. Numbness is a symptom too."

Numbness is a symptom of post-traumatic stress disorder. Holding the phone to my ear, I sat there, literally unable to speak. Maybe I wasn't a cold, uncaring person. Maybe I had been touched by what had happened to you after all. The detachment I'd carried with so much shame through the decades was actually bereavement at work. Just as cerebral palsy dulled sensation in my body, grief dulled my emotions over all you had suffered and all I had lost.

While Joseph waited on the other end of the line, I closed my eyes and felt something grow quiet inside me, like a still body of water. Like the hushed bay around the corner from our childhood home.

Chapter Thirty-Five

In the days after I finished reading the trial transcripts, I went over my notes. When I came upon the Mendez-Arline Exclusionary Rule, I googled it, seeking a clear description of the statute that was used to dismiss the alternative explanation defense.

"This rule, in plain English, requires that anyone who wishes to present a 'Third Party Culpability' defense - in other words, 'I didn't do it, it was someone else' - must present sufficient evidence to sustain a conviction against the third party."

I found this definition on an alternative news site called *Steamshovel*, in a 1999 article titled, "A Brief, Yet Helpful Guide to Amerika's Eugenic Courts: Class Warfare for Beginners." The author takes issue with the ruling, going on to say, "It's not bloody likely that the judge will, in fact, rule in your favor - even if you're able to produce overwhelming evidence - as it is not in the judge's best interests to rule against the Gestapo..."

Something felt wrong with the way this article was written. The author seemed knowledgeable enough, but why all the snark and vitriol?

Scrolling back to the beginning, I stared at his picture, long hair tossed over one broad shoulder, shirt unbuttoned almost to the waist. I glanced at the bizarre title, complete with the Kafka K of an angsty, adolescent writer, and finally caught sight of the byline. Wayne Henderson.

The room swayed, and my skin grew warm and prickly. It was Philip. Bill Fazio had told me he'd once read some kind of blog by your killer, and I'd searched for it unsuccessfully, not having thought to look under Philip's middle name. Now that it had found me, I felt edgy and afraid, and I couldn't shake the sense of being watched. As though Philip could be two places at once, locked three thousand miles away in Mule Creek Prison and here in this room with his stolen rifle and crosscut bullets, his rabid temper, and the one-percent tattoo that marked him as proudly on the lunatic fringe.

Months before meeting Bill and receiving the transcripts, I'd read what little I could find about the Hendersons on the Internet. A search for Velma had led to a beautifully produced PDF pamphlet on the rough conditions aging women face in the California prison system. *Dignity Denied*, by Heidi Strupp and Donna Willmott, described how difficult it was for these inmates to get proper medical care, how long they had to wait for eyeglasses and other prescriptions, and how vulnerable they were to the violence around them.

"The continued incarceration of frail elders – who represent the smallest threat to public safety but the largest cost to incarcerate – embodies failed public policy."

Quotes by inmates were peppered throughout the publication, reproduced in what appeared to be their own handwriting. Velma wasn't quoted, but she was pictured, smiling warmly, the harshness I remembered in her face softened away by age. Could a woman who had aided in such vicious murders have turned gentle in prison, I wondered as I studied the small, posed photo. I thought of a documentary I'd seen about a writing workshop the playwright Eve Ensler, now known as V, once led in a woman's penitentiary. The participants, many of whom had committed violent crimes years before, were candid and articulate. Had Velma ever sat in a room like that, reflecting on the cruel and desperate person she'd once been? I stopped myself there. The pamphlet had been crafted to elicit sympathy for its subjects, and I was its target audience. Watcher of documentaries on PBS. Guilt-prone, tenderhearted liberal with a credit card in reach. I slammed my laptop closed, feeling sullied and manipulated. *Dignity Denied* offered no mention in its elegant pages of why those women found themselves in a maximum-security prison, no acknowledgement of what any of them had done.

By googling Philip, I'd learned that, upon his imprisonment, he'd petitioned to keep his hair long, claiming that cutting it would violate his spiritual beliefs. I'd also discovered that he'd been briefly considered for release in 1985, along with over a thousand other suspects of "San Francisco's worst crimes," due to alleged mishandling of computer files by the police. Among the breached documents were Philip's psychological evaluations and children's service agency records, including those from a residential treatment center for emotionally disturbed teenagers.

Now, here he was—half of the maniacal pair who strangled you, suffocated Ray-Ray, executed Ray with a gun to the head—sounding off in a rag described in *Wikipedia* as "a zine devoted to conspiracy theories and parapolitics."

"The first fact that must be internalized is this: PIGS LIE..." Philip wrote in this tale of how he and Velma were framed by the entire judicial system, and I couldn't help noting his use of the epithet favored by mass murderer Charles Manson.

Now that I knew his pen name, I found another of his articles, published in January 2000, on a site called *Justice Denied*, "The Magazine for the Wrongly Convicted." By a chilling coincidence, the piece was edited, though clearly not vetted, by a woman named Clara A. Thomas Boggs.

Philip is pictured twice: cross-legged with his hands in a peaceful mudra, and in that same *GQ*-like portrait used in *Steamshovel*. His drawings are there too, self-portraits in a 1970's-album-cover style. In one, he plays a flute while shackled to the prison gates. I stared at it, working to slow my ragged breathing before moving on to his words.

"CONSIDER THIS...You've been traveling cross-country, just a leisurely 'working vacation' by car: you stop in San Francisco, and agree to split rent, temporarily, with what seems like a nice young couple. Unfortunately, it turns out that the 'nice young couple' have criminal records, are selling crank... owe a major chunk of change to local biker gangs. In the meantime, your car has been towed for a parking violation, you're strapped for cash to get it out of hock, and death-threats from the biker stepuglies are flying as thick as divorce lawyers in Tijuana."

In his version, you and Ray gave him your *broken-down* panel truck to thank him for splitting the rent and paying your pizza bills.

"It's beyond obvious that we weren't even in California when the murders occurred, and wouldn't have any reason to kill people who, for whatever faults they might've had, certainly knew how to party."

It's beyond obvious, he claimed, because "The Frisco police themselves proved our whereabouts...we were in Reno, Nevada at 1:30PM, on 12 January 1982, 24 hours before one of our alleged victims spoke to the landlord on the phone."

By now I felt physically ill, my heart beating too hard at each glaring omission. How it was established that you'd made that call on the 11th. How the police *proved their whereabouts* by following a breadcrumb trail of all the things they'd stolen from you, including one of the murder weapons.

This is what evil really sounds like, I thought, my eyes stinging with tears. It's self-righteous and sarcastic, even as it tells outright lies. It's in love with its own smarmy voice.

The image of Ray hog-tied, that had haunted me since my conversation with Ilyas, came to me now in stark relief. Ray knew, in those final torturous moments, what they'd done to you and Ray-Ray that morning. I felt sure of it. Once the Hendersons had him bound and helpless, Philip boasted in the same cocky voice he used on the page, forcing Ray to picture every gory and savage detail before they shut off his mind for good.

They relished it, Angie, or at least he did. Everything points to that. Crosscutting the bullets, tying up Ray like a beast. For Philip, murder was a labor of love.

"It's unbelievable what people do to each other," Ilyas had said to me on the phone, which recalls the last line of a poem by Carolyn Forché I'd memorized years before. *There is nothing one man will not do to another.* The poem, published the year before you were killed, is about that dark time in El Salvador when citizens were tortured and murdered by dictators installed by our government. Now, for me, it would forever also be about the pleasure Philip clearly took in his own heinous acts.

"... we were still able to amass enough evidence to prove our innocence, ... and all our evidence was invariably excluded by a 'prosecution friendly' judge."

"Invariably excluded," I repeated, reeling from how blithely Philip excluded that one of his victims was pregnant and another was an eleven-month-old baby. Nowhere in either of his articles does he acknowledge that Ray-Ray ever existed.

Five years after I discovered those articles, Philip would die in prison at sixty. Four years after that, during a global pandemic, eighty-six-year-old Velma would be resentenced to her thirty-eight years served and released. In brief letters to Terry Boggs and me, she'd reiterate Philip's bullshit story.

"... I was present when Ray was attached [sic] by a member of a Hawaiian bike club. I was shaken by this and other dealings with bikers while living there. I was very scared of this type of person and was urging my husband that we return home."

Did she think we weren't aware of all the evidence against them? What did she hope to gain by lying now that Philip was dead, and she was out on the parole her original sentence had promised would never be possible? Unless she'd actually come to believe their fabrications. If shame could wipe so much from my memory, maybe the horror of her own actions could do the same to hers.

Regardless, back on the night I first read Philip's ravings online, I lay in bed haunted by your final morning, variations of the scene playing in a loop while I tried to sleep. Sometimes, it was Philip you argued with in silent movie pantomime while Velma snuck up behind you with that yellow towel. Sometimes, the Hendersons switched places. Over and over, you lost your footing and tripped out of your slipper as you fell to the floor, the breath squeezed out of you as your lovely hands batted at air.

"I don't blame the Hendersons for what happened to Andra," Cousin Lauren had told me months earlier. "I blame your parents. They set her on a course that made her put herself in danger constantly."

Had I heard that even a year before she and I reconnected, I might have been shocked. But after all I'd learned about our parents' choices, there was no denying that they'd made your life miserable and precarious in ways I'd never truly comprehend. And, in truth, I had never really blamed the Hendersons either. While I didn't doubt the fact of their guilt, they, like so much else, had never seemed quite real to me. I'd thought of them the way I thought of the car that hit our friend and neighbor Lisa in the street. An inanimate force. Mere props in the tragic end to your story.

But now that I'd read Philip's lies and invectives, I understood in my body what he and Velma had done. The two of them ruthlessly ended your evolving, imperfect, promising life. They did the same to Ray, to little Ray-Ray, and to the flawlessly formed baby girl who was just weeks away from taking her first breath. The Hendersons killed you with brutality and calculation and not a moment's remorse. It took me thirty years to feel enraged about it, but now my cold hands shook while my face burned as though lit from within, and my jaw clamped down so hard I could practically feel my back teeth turning to powder. And, while I never would have thought my fury could do any good, the emotion was so intense, so long overdue and right in this instance, it broke me open.

Over the next few nights, as I lay waiting for sleep, I continued to see flashes of you struggling with the Hendersons in a losing battle for your life. But soon, other images came to me too. I recalled the smoothness of your cheek against mine as we posed for photos, saw your smile twisting as you held back a laugh, and felt the brush of your slender fingers as you poked playfully at my ribs. Pulling the blankets tightly around me, I missed you terribly and discovered that allowing myself to feel it was actually a way to have you near.

Chapter Thirty-Six

One gray afternoon, toward the end of my research trip to California, I rode down an industrial strip in Colma, a town known in the Bay Area as the City of the Dead. Naomi was driving, Gracie beside her in the front seat. While Tina and I had never managed to find our way to each other in her lifetime, my love for her children is fierce and uncomplicated. This was why, as I sat behind her daughters on that brief drive—listening to their easy banter, noticing how often they touched—I didn't feel jealous the way I often did around sisters. Instead, their intimacy seemed to infuse the air with extra oxygen. It signified something in our family that had gone right.

I remembered how, when Dad was in the hospital in the last days of his life, he'd turned an accusing eye to me and yelled, "Do you think I wanted only one child?" He was mad that I hadn't gotten there earlier in the morning. That, with a five-year-old at home, I hadn't gotten there more often through the week. "I have amazing nieces and nephews," I'd felt tempted to say as I straightened his covers and offered him a sip of water from the cup on his bedside table. "They'd all be your grandchildren if you had opened your heart."

Now, while two of those grandchildren continued to chat in the front seat on our way to find your grave, I wondered if, had Dad been capable of loving Mom's children as his own, she'd have been able to love you in turn. If you were watched over and cherished as I had been, you wouldn't have felt such an urgent need to escape, which means you wouldn't have had to figure out, while still a child, how to survive on your own. In all likelihood, you'd have stayed home long enough to finish school. What's more, you'd have moved through the world with a belief in yourself that can only come from knowing how valued you'd always been.

"What did I do to deserve you?" Mom used to ask me as a kind of overflow. Angie, I wish more than anything that you could have had that. And yet, by this point in my exploration, I'd come to believe that, even as our parents made their most damaging choices, they were more ignorant than malicious. Our cousin Lois had recently told me that, when Dad called to let her mother know about the murders, he confided to Aunt Bess, "We did something wrong while raising Andra, but I can't put my finger on how it began." Mom, too, must have managed not to recognize her own harmful role in your brief life. After all, back when I first became a mother myself, she essentially suggested I write this book.

"I think this is it," Naomi said as we turned onto a small road that proved to be a wide driveway. We were in Woodlawn Memorial Park, a place I'd learned the name of only months before when your death certificate had arrived in the mail.

Inside the office, the groundskeeper thumbed through a drawer of index cards.

"Boggs, Boggs..." she murmured until she hit upon the right yellowed rectangle. "Looks like they were cremated and buried together in one plot."

Moments later, we pulled up to a field of white stones shaped like archways, all identical, all military graves. Naomi, who held the map the groundskeeper had given us, led us to the site. There was only one name engraved on the stone.

Raymond M Boggs Jr.
US Army
Vietnam
1949 - 1982

Only Ray's family had cared enough to arrange a burial and mark the grave, a fact that made me feel like I shouldn't even be there. Like I didn't deserve to sit on that hallowed patch of ground. Still, I found solace in knowing that you, Ray, and your children all shared the same small space. It made your death seem less lonely somehow. I sank onto the grass, and our nieces sat on either side of me, close enough that our knees touched, making this pilgrimage less lonely too.

"Look." I pointed to four field daisies poking out of the grass.

"One for each life," Gracie said.

"Do you have anything of Angie's to remember her by?" Naomi asked.

"Two delicate gold rings," I said and, after a moment, admitted why I felt bad about having them.

"You know, Angie lost a ring of our mom's," Gracie said. "A jade ring."

"Seems like there were a lot of rings in Angie's story," Naomi observed.

Our nieces—Gracie who, two-years-old at the time of your death, intuited that something had gone wrong in the world and cried inconsolably the entire day; Naomi who was born just six days after your body was found—knew about the ring that was held as evidence in the Henderson trial. Now, I told them about the gumball machine diamond Ray gave you the day after you met, and the wedding set I read about in the transcripts that you bought from Rose so our parents and I would think you and Ray were officially married. I even described a ring you never knew about; one my ex-husband had asked me to have inked onto my finger to prove my love to him. I couldn't do it, couldn't ever get a tattoo knowing Philip Henderson was covered in them.

Sighing, I peeled a ring off my finger. Such a small thing, a little circle of silver framing a hole. But small things were all I'd ever been able to give you. I could keep your smoking a secret. Swap my leather jacket for your frayed sweater, knowing you'd gotten the better deal. Be the one person in the family who was always thrilled to see you. Except for that last time when, not knowing it would be the last time, I allowed myself to feel restless and superior.

"Sometimes we'd trade things," I said, burying the ring.

After we covered the spot with pebbles, Naomi asked if I'd like time alone. I nodded, and she and Gracie dusted off their jeans and left to wait in the car.

"Hey, Ray," I whispered, touching the grooves of his name. "Thank you for being so loving to my sister."

Next, I talked to Ray-Ray, telling him what a good baby he was, and to your daughter who never made it to birth. "I wish you had seen the sky and that you'd gotten to be a little sister. It's the best."

Finally, I spoke to you, my first love in this life.

"Remember how you once apologized for not being a better sister? Well, really, that was me. I could have been a better sister. I'm so sorry."

Wiping away my tears, I thought of reciting the Mourner's Kaddish, but the image that came to me with those ancient words was of the two of us dancing on our twin beds with pajama bottoms on our heads. I sang a verse of "I'm a Believer" instead.

Before we left the cemetery, I stopped at the office where I filled out a form and pulled out my credit card. It wasn't until we were halfway back to Oakland that I realized I should have consulted Ray's brothers before arranging to alter the stone.

As soon as I was settled back home in Hoboken, I phoned Terry Boggs.

"You know how the headstone only has Ray's name..." I started.

"What happened was, my mom got the VA to engrave it before the other bodies were found," he explained. "We couldn't afford to change it, but it bothered me. If Angie does have family, I thought, how will they find her? How will they know she's there?

"You thought that?" I felt my throat close up at the kindness. "So, I guess you won't mind. I went ahead and arranged to have the other names added."

"Mind?" Terry started to cry. "I always wished I had the money to do that."

Two months later, I received a letter from Woodlawn Memorial Park saying the work was completed. I called Terry who drove to Colma that same afternoon and took a picture of the headstone with his phone. All through that evening, I stole peeks at it.

Raymond M Boggs Jr.
US Army
Vietnam
1949 - 1982
Angie
1956 - 1982
Raymond M III
1981 - 1982
Baby Unborn

"That's sad," Ethan said when I showed him the photo.

Of course it was heartbreaking, a gravestone for an entire family who had died violently. At the same time, I also saw it as a kind of mending. So much had been withheld and taken from you in your brief life, and I'd been incapable of doing anything about it. Now, finally, I'd figured out a way to stand up for you, and soon I'd do it again by writing our story. I'd say that I remember. I'd mark that you were here.

Acknowledgements

A secretive family is, by nature and necessity, an isolated one. The flipside to that, I discovered through the many years of researching and writing this book, is that the very acts of truth-seeking and truth-telling draw people to you, and you to them. For this I am forever grateful.

I'll start, as this story does, in California. Naomi Ages, you are the beating heart of our family. Thank you, foremost, for inviting me back into the fold, and for housing me during my return to the Bay Area to learn what I could of Angie's life there. You provided a nurturing place for me to come home to each evening after making heartbreaking, sometimes gruesome, discoveries. Herman Seidell and Sarvaga Grace Antrobus, thank you for accompanying me on parts of that journey. What a gift to have you by my side. I'm deeply thankful to your father, Howard Seidell, too, for filling me in on Angie's early days in San Francisco and, beyond that, for being such a gentle and loving presence in my life and in our family. I wish he were here with us now.

Kay Vorhies, thank you for being with me on Angie, Ray, and little Ray-Ray's last day, for remembering what I couldn't, and for discouraging me from riding off on the back of that motorcycle all those years ago. Here's to more than four decades of friendship so far.

Bill Fazio, enormous gratitude to you for prosecuting the murder case so brilliantly and for your graciousness and generosity in the years since. May every suffering family have as skilled and compassionate an ally as you.

Thank you, Judge Harry Dorfman, for caring about my family's story and tracking down thirty-year-old transcripts for me.

Ilyas Absar, your kindness to Angie and Ray when they lived on Webster Street means so much to me, as does your kindness to me when we spoke.

Deep appreciation to you, Joseph Boggs. I'm so glad we connected. You taught me a lot, not just about Ray, but about me.

And Terry Boggs, thank God for you. My openhearted brother, my mirror in this loss, thank you for showing me I don't have to carry it alone.

Napoleon Hendrix and Prentice Earl Sanders, when I had the chance, I didn't thank you nearly enough for how hard you worked on my family's behalf. Deepest gratitude to you both, in memoriam, for solving the crime so quickly and ingeniously and for all your remarkable work in the service of justice.

Gratitude and love, again in memoriam, to my Aunt Helen Sbar and my cousin Lauren Eichelbaum. When I needed to find you, you were each right there. When I needed the truth, you each shared it openly. I wish I'd had you longer. I can't believe you're gone.

To the cousins I call Rachel and Lois, I can't tell you how much it meant to me to hear about Angie's life before my birth. Your openness helped me understand our family in new and necessary ways.

I am amazed and grateful to you, Jimmie Bay, for sharing your extraordinary gift with me. Your insights broke me open.

My childhood friends, Marianne Hodgins and Aviva Weintraub, thank you for sharing your memories with me and giving me so many good ones of my own.

Thank you, Daniel Un, for answering my questions about

Hartman Home and for saving my embarrassing poems and love notes, circa 1976. They helped me recapture my teenage voice. Thank you, too, to the man I refer to as *Andra's crush*. Your candor was so helpful and your kindness so appreciated. We Gritz sisters clearly had good taste in boys, given what mensches you two grew up to be.

To the schoolmate I refer to as Marnie, I so appreciate your frankness and generosity in sharing your experiences at Spofford and Hartman Home with me.

Nina Bernstein, your research and writing on The New York State Training School for Girls opened the door to my understanding of Angie's life outside our childhood home and the damaged juvenile justice and foster care system she was thrust into. I'm very grateful for your work.

Thank you, Shar Hale, for entrusting me with your thoughts and memories of the Training School.

To the staff at The San Francisco Public Library, Driscoll's Mortuary Chapel, The Hudson Area Public Library, The New York Public Library, The New York City Health Department, The New York State Archives, P.S. 104, and Scholar's Academy, I wish I'd learned your names. I'm very grateful to you.

Gratitude and admiration to you, Alison Cornyn, founder of the Incorrigibles Project. I'm so moved by how you use art to help women and girls who were and are unjustly incarcerated, and so honored that you've invited me to share in that work. I continue to learn from you and the community of lovely, resilient women you've brought together. Cynthia Boykin, Trish Howard, Kathleen Hulser, and Lily Perez, thank you.

Andi Buchanan and Dawn Raffel, writing comrades in my two home cities, I'm so grateful to have each of you to commiserate and celebrate with when we come up out of our dens for air. Your voices on the page and across cafe tables inspire and invigorate me. Thank you both for the love you've shown to me and to this book.

Thank you, Kay Leroy, for generously allowing me to hold a thirty-year memorial for Angie, Ray, and Ray-Ray in your home.

Hettie Jones, my first memoir teacher, your encouragement and example mean the world to this fellow Far Rock High alum.

Beth Kephart, thank you for your Sunday memoir workshops, your many kindnesses to me, and your many gorgeous books. They confirmed for me that it's more than okay to remain a poet while writing in prose.

Rachel Simon, this book was a seedling in my imagination when our friendship began. Thank you for all the ways you encouraged it into being, and for the example of your own beautiful writing on having and being a sister.

Jane Bernstein, your exquisite memoir, *Bereft*, helped me begin to understand my own unreachable feelings and slowly find my way toward them. It also allowed me to see that sharing Angie's and my story in this way was not only possible, but necessary. I'm truly grateful to you for writing it and truly sorry for your loss.

Helen Fremont, thank you for showing me through the example of your stunning books that painful, complex family stories can be told artfully and with love. Your warmth and generosity have made this enamored fan feel like an enamored friend.

Gratitude to you, Sue William Silverman, for being the fearless and lovely writer and person you are. Your memoirs and essays have fed and riveted me, and my copy of *Fearless Confessions* is marked with exclamation points. Its wisdom, your wisdom, guided the many drafts of this book.

Thank you, Rosalie Brereton, Hope DeRogatis, Barbara Falcone, Henry Goldschlag (in memoriam), Nava Hall, Julia Hough, Anne Kaier, Rachel Maizes, Ellen Rosenblatt, Nina

Schafer, Miriam Seidel, Wendy Setzer, Aita Susi, J.C. Todd, Diana Ward, Dave Worrell, and Amy Zuelch for championing this project and supporting me, each in your own loving way.

Jennie Dunham, you always wanted the best for this book, and I could always feel it. Thank you.

So much gratitude to the writers and friends who've read my manuscript (in some cases, more than once) and helped me make it its best possible self: Andrea J. Buchanan, Ann Hood, Kimberly Behre Kenna, Alina MacNeal, Deb Oestreicher, Georgia Popoff, Dawn Raffel, and Sue Repko.

Lilly Dancyger, thank you especially. Through your remarkable class, Creating a Narrative Arc Out of a Messy Life, and your supremely gifted editing, you guided me in uncovering the shape of *Everywhere I Look* and its emotional center. I also learned so much from your own fiercely beautiful writing on grief and discovery in *Negative Space*.

Kevin Atticks, MK Barnes, Lindsey Bonavita, Ariana Mera, and Jack Stromberg, my wonderful team at Apprentice House Press. I'm so grateful to you for choosing to bring this book out into the world and for doing so with such openness, attention, and care.

Shirley Brewer, fellow poet and beloved friend, I can't thank you enough for introducing Apprentice House Press and me to each other. Through your generosity and stellar matchmaking skills, you made my most cherished wish come true.

To my mother-in-law Miriam Dell in memoriam, and my sisters-in-law, Kathy Kiggins and Connie Hovis: I came into your family orphaned, and you made me yours. What an incredible gift!

Dan Simpson, my first reader, my best friend, and the love of my life, I never would have had the courage to go back into my heartbreaking past if I didn't have your steadfast love to come home to.

Ethan Gilbert, you have your aunt's impish smile and her sly humor, together with your own golden heart and unstoppable brilliance. How I got lucky enough to be your mother, I'll never know. I'm eternally grateful.

Gratitude, in memoriam, to Raymond Martin Boggs, Jr. for loving Angie so well and being so patient and kind to teenage me, and to Raymond Martin Boggs III for being wonderful you.

And, finally, Angie Boggs, the first person I remember loving, it's all here in these pages. I hope I came close to doing you justice. Damn, I miss you.

About the Author

Ona Gritz holds a Master of Arts in poetry from the creative writing program at New York University. She is the author, most recently, of *August Or Forever*, a Reader's Choice and Wishing Shelf finalist in middle grade fiction. Ona's nonfiction has appeared in *Brevity*, *The Guardian*, *The New York Times*, *River Teeth*, *The Rumpus*, *The Utne Reader*, and been named Notable in *The Best American Essays* and Best of the Year in *Salon*. Her earlier books include *On the Whole: A Story of Mothering and Disability* and *Geode*, a finalist for the Main Street Rag Poetry Book Award. She won the Poetry Archive Now Worldview 2020 Competition and has received many other honors for her poems, which have been widely anthologized. Ona lives with her husband, writer Daniel Simpson, near Philadelphia.

Sources

Ambrosino, Lillian. *Runaways*. Beacon Press, 1971.

Bernstein, Nina. "Punishing Women, Punishing Girls." *Alicia Patterson Foundation*, 1996.

Bernstein, Nina. "Ward of the State: The Gap in Ella Fitzgerald's Life." *New York Times*, 23 Jun. 1996.

Bernstein, Nina. *The Lost Children of Wilder: The Epic Struggle to Change Foster Care*. Vintage Books, 2002.

Feldman, Bruce and Joseph Sargent. *Maybe I'll Come Home in the Spring*. ABC Movie of the Week, 16 Feb. 1971.

Foote, Jennifer. "Florida Holds Couple Wanted in Slaughter of S.F. Family." *San Francisco Examiner*, 30 April, 1982.

Forché, Carolyn. "The Visitor." *The Country Between Us*. Harper & Row, 1981.

Giallombardo, Rose Mary. *The Social World of Imprisoned Girls: a Comparative Study of Institutions for Juvenile Delinquents*. John Wiley & Sons, 1974.

Henderson, Wayne. "A Brief, Yet Helpful Guide To Amerika's Eugenic Courts." *Steamshovel Press*, 1999.

Kaysen, Susanna. *Girl Interrupted*. Vintage Books, 1994.

Maaz, Larry. "S.F. Police Have Not a Clue About Three Neatly Wrapped Bodies." *San Francisco Examiner*, 20, Mar, 1982.

Oelsner, Lesley. "Juvenile Justice: Helpless Frustration." *New York Times*, 3 Apr. 1973.

Oelsner, Lesley. "Juvenile Justice: Failures in the System of Detention." *New York Times*, 4 Apr. 1973.

Oelsner, Lesley. "Juvenile Justice: Search for Reform." *New York Times*, 5 Apr. 1973.

Oelsner, Lesley. "City to Shut Shelter And Jail for Girls 'Within the Year'." *New York Times*, 17 Apr. 1973.

Olsen, Tillie. *Tell Me a Riddle*. Dell Publishing Co./Laurel Edition, 1981.

Opatrny, Dennis J. "Coroner's Evidence Could Link Couple to Family's Murder." *San Francisco Examiner*, 1 Dec, 1982.

Peters, William. "The Riddle of Teenage Runaways." *Good Housekeeping*, Jun. 1968.

Sibley, John. "Youth Problems Restudied in Light of Oswald Case." *New York Times*, 5 Jan. 1964.

Strupp Heidi and Donna Willmott. *Dignity Denied: The Price of Imprisoning Older Women in California*. Legal Services for Prisoners with Children, 2004.

Teltsch, Kathleen. "City Acting to Reform Its Youth Detention Facilities." *New York Times*, 22 Sept. 1968.

Thompson, A.C. "Scary San Francisco: Six Places Where Bad Things Happened." *San Francisco Bay Guardian*, 23 Apr, 2003.

White, Welsh S. *Litigating in the Shadow of Death: Defense Attorneys in Capital Cases*. University of Michigan, 2006.

Wooden, Kenneth. *Weeping in the Playtime of Others: America's Incarcerated Children*. McGraw-Hill, 1976.

Zamora, Jim Herron. "S.F.'s Top Sleuth Calls It Quits After 34 Years." *San Francisco Gate*, 12 Sept. 1999.

"Body Found Rolled Up in Rug." *San Francisco Chronicle*. 1 Mar, 1982.

"Two More Bodies Found Under House in S.F." *San Francisco Chronicle*, 20 Mar, 1982.

"Fine Sleuthing Solves S.F. Murders of 3." *San Francisco Examiner*, 30, Apr, 1982.

People v. Henderson, 225 Cal. App. 3d 1129 (1990).

"Wayne Henderson." *Justice Denied*, Volume 1, issue 10, Jan, 2000.

Credits

A version of Chapter 26 of this memoir was published as "Seeking Pauline" in *Full Grown People*, October 25, 2016.

Essays related to this story appear in the following publications:

Brain Child, Brevity, Cutbank Literary Magazine, Lunch Ticket, The New York Times, The Rumpus, Salon, Thread, and *The Truth of Memoir* by Kerry Cohen, Writer's Digest Books, 2014.

Some were reprinted in my chapbook, *Present Imperfect,* Poets Wear Prada, 2021.

I wrote these essays while working on this book and occasionally cross-pollinated sentences.

Apprentice
House Press
Loyola University Maryland

Apprentice House is the country's only campus-based, student-staffed book publishing company. Directed by professors and industry professionals, it is a nonprofit activity of the Communication Department at Loyola University Maryland.

Using state-of-the-art technology and an experiential learning model of education, Apprentice House publishes books in untraditional ways. This dual responsibility as publishers and educators creates an unprecedented collaborative environment among faculty and students, while teaching tomorrow's editors, designers, and marketers.

Eclectic and provocative, Apprentice House titles intend to entertain as well as spark dialogue on a variety of topics. Financial contributions to sustain the press's work are welcomed. Contributions are tax deductible to the fullest extent allowed by the IRS.

To learn more about Apprentice House books or to obtain submission guidelines, please visit www.apprenticehouse.com.

Apprentice House Press
Communication Department
Loyola University Maryland
4501 N. Charles Street
Baltimore, MD 21210
Ph: 410-617-5265
info@apprenticehouse.com • www.apprenticehouse.com